GANGLAND
TO GUINEA

NEW ZEALAND, SIERRA LEONE AND A REMARKABLE TRUE STORY

HUW DONALDSON

ARK
house

Ark House Press
arkhousepress.com

Cataloguing in Publication Data:
Title: Gangland to Guinea
ISBN: 978-1-7640298-0-3 (pbk)
Subjects: [REL012170]   RELIGION / Christian Living / Personal Memoirs; [REL012040]   RELIGION / Christian Living / Inspirational; [BIO018000] BIOGRAPHY & AUTOBIOGRAPHY / Religious;

Design by initiateagency.com

CONTENTS

CHAPTER 1

FOR AS LONG AS ANYONE CAN REMEMBER

The tattoos on my arm speak of a dark and violent past, but that is not the way my life began.

It started back in 1978. My parents, Alan and Catherine Donaldson had been married for several years already and I was the third and last of the children to be born into our family. My brother, James, was three at the time and my sister, Beth, was two. Dad was an engineer and worked for his father's engineering company. Mum had a master's degree in English and played the viola in the Christchurch Symphony Orchestra. At this stage we were living in Sumner, a suburb on the eastern side of the city of Christchurch in the South Island of New Zealand. Christchurch in 1978 was a great place to raise a family. The city had a population of just over 290,000 and presented beautiful scenes on all fronts. We had the beaches and coastal areas in the east, plus magnificent steep hills and pockets of native bush all over Banks Peninsula on that same coastal front. On the outskirts of the city to the South, West and North is some of the best flat agricultural land in the South Island. Canterbury as the region is called, has always been a productive area although the district has been through some tough times including drought, earthquakes and economic challenges. Further to the west the Southern Alps rise out of the edges of the Canterbury plains and at the right time of the year, when the sky is clear, you can see all the way across the plains to the snow-capped Alps. The first memories I have of Christchurch are obviously from a few years after 1978. In fact, we only stayed in Sumner for a short time before my parents rented out our Sumner house to tenants and we all moved over to a place called Little River on Banks Peninsula. My parents thought it would be great to bring up their children in a rural setting and since Little River wasn't too far out, being only an hour's drive from Christchurch, and a really beautiful part of Canterbury, that's where we ended up.

My first memories are from Little River. We lived there from not long after I was born until about 1984. If you look on the map of New Zealand you can see a straight coastline that comes down the eastern side of the South Island and just about in line with Christchurch city, Banks Peninsula protrudes out into the ocean. It is quite large and, if you are traveling from the Port Hills which lie alongside the eastern side of Christchurch City out to the furthest point on the peninsula, it would take you a couple of hours driving with a few hilly bits along the way. Little River lies right in the middle with very steep hills on both sides. There is a scattering of native bush on most of the faces with some heavier pockets in and around the valleys. We lived in Okuti Valley. A beautiful quiet spot dotted with stands of trees and a constant chorus from the bird life. Okuti was about five minutes out from Little River and, as it was off the main road, it was just that little bit better if you were looking for that totally secluded rural setting. Back in those days you weren't considered a local until you'd lived there for twenty years or more and we of course had only just moved into the area, so we were considered townies to the locals. This is where I can recall my first memories though. Good times, Dad was there, a big strong man of solid stature and a beard. A quiet man from what I can remember but I know everybody liked him and I've been told he did like a good conversation. He would talk to people, even strangers on the side of the road. Dad liked fishing and classical music. One time I remember, I must have only been three or four years old, we were pulling the old dry corn plants and other material out of the vegetable garden and around the house and putting them onto a big bonfire. Along with cups full of petrol dad would fling them onto the already burning bonfire. Due to my young age and size it seemed like the flames went forever up into the sky. Dad was big and so was the fire. I can remember the rain in Little River too. When it rains there it really buckets down. When you were inside the house, which was an old weatherboard house with a corrugated iron roof, you could really hear the rain thundering down on the roof. I just remember the sensation of being in there and it was cosy, safe and we were all there. There's not a lot of memories because we only stayed there for about five years before moving back into town, but I can remember snippets. Giant earth worms in the soil outside that could have been up to fifteen centimetres long. I remember having a store down our long drive which comprised a box and a few totally worthless items on top that we three children were trying to sell. I'm not sure but I think someone may have given us two cents for something in the stand on this particular afternoon. We young ones were convinced that a witch lived nearby. Obviously, an imaginary witch who we believed was there. I don't recall a lot about this particular witch, but I think she lived off to the side under the thick dark undergrowth. I'm sure we could have told you some scary things about her at the time, but it's a little too long ago now to recall the exact details about her. Maybe she was just there at night when we were trying to go to sleep. Some of the things I can remember are amazing when I think about them. My brother and I got chased by a mothering pig one day. We were aware of the sow and her litter in amongst the undergrowth not far from our house. Having stalked her through the bushes, we poked our noses around the corner to look at them, and the pig grunted and quickly headed towards us. We ran and didn't look back until we got to the safety of the fence alongside the drive to our house where we went through the wire and back to safety.

The people back then were all so interesting too. At that young age the adults were the bosses and a lot more. Almost as if they were a different species to us. Amazing, towering people who looked after us. Some of them looked after us anyway. My nana would have been there, and our grandparents on my mother's side also visited us. My mother's family were of Welsh ancestry; both grandparents on that side were actually born in Wales. And on my father's side if you went back far enough, the Donaldson family, my grandfather's family, we know came from Scotland. Dad's mother had various ideas about her ancestry that also included French and English, but we don't know exactly, there may have been other interesting backgrounds in the Stacey family. Nana seemed to think that there was Jewish ancestry as well. Because of my mother's Welsh parents she had lovely jet-black hair and fine features. Dad was a very handsome man with lovely olive skin and brown hair. Looking back at photos it's easy to see why my mother liked him. Likewise, my mother was definitely beautiful as well. I can also recall another woman called Julia, who was an old family friend from Australia. Julia smoked cigarettes and was thin with long, curly, dark hair, a pale complexion and a roman nose. I liked her a lot. We only had her stay with us the one time though, after that I never saw her again. Another person who was there was the farmer who owned our house. One time I recall being on the bulldozer with him, and we were walking the crawler down a farm track. I also recall a strange female babysitter who looked after us one night too, because Dad and mum must have been at an orchestra event and, well, yes that was a fairly strange memory. I would say that she became a little excited at being left alone with us and for whatever reason she began to exhibit what I would now consider to be sexualised behaviour. I know a bit later my Mum and Dad came home, with mum wearing her long dark, formal gown. I recall the babysitter's startled reaction as my parents pulled up the drive and I remember her attempting to quickly correct herself as if she had been caught in the middle of something, which obviously she had been. There has been some speculation among us as to what went on that night but I'm the only one who can remember the incident.

Overall though, I think mainly it's the presence of people that sticks; for me it's the fact that I know they were there. My sister Beth for example, I know she was there. My dad sitting in the lounge overlooking the valley listening to classical music with all of us present. I think for a young boy in his first years it would have been a happy time. What more could a boy have asked for? To be there with his family and with a world of adventure out there waiting to be explored.

According to my mother, we left there around 1984 because the farmer John Waller wanted to put the house on the market. Which makes sense because I was wondering about the release date of the Billy Joel song "The Longest Time", and apparently it was 1984. For some reason I distinctly remember that great old song on the radio in the car with mum and us children, "Oh, oh, oh, oh, for the longest time", I like that song to this day. We moved back to our Sumner house for a short period of time. Mum said we were only in Sumner for a couple of months and then as far as I know we moved to Halswell which is on the edges of Christchurch, but still rural. We would have stayed in Halswell for a short time before moving to Rolleston, twenty-five minutes' drive from Christchurch where Dad and Mum purchased a five-acre lifestyle block. It was a long narrow property on an unsealed road with a front paddock and a shingle drive leading up the side of the paddock to our Frae Mohs built home. Behind the house was a garage, then a yard, a workshop and hay barn with a farm track that led out to the back paddocks and pine trees at the back of the property. Rolleston is dry and flat. It's all part of a centuries old riverbed that used to run through the area, so the ground was hard and stony. To this day it still seems beautiful to me, with great big blue gums that have stood the test of time in hot or cold dotted along the side of the road swaying backwards and forwards in the breeze. On a clear day you could see the mountains off in the distance. The pine trees at the back of the property added a little adventure for us young ones whenever we wanted to go exploring. There were sheep in the paddocks, magpies flying overhead and horses as a constant friend of my sister and mother who used to love them. We had Welsh Mountain Ponies but there were other horses at various other properties along the road. Rolleston became probably the most prominent memory among my childhood recollections. For me it was our family home where we all lived together, before dad passed away. Dad spent his last years with us at that property and it was the final period we were together in happy times as a family. Most of what I know of my dad was from Rolleston.

During that time while my dad was alive, I watched him go to work every day. We used to go to school and we would only see him in the evenings and on the weekends. Dad had a company 4wd which we used to go and source firewood from time to time. Other things we did together was going fishing, watching westerns and war movies on the television and doing small chores around the property. Mum would take us children to church on Sundays, but after some time I managed to get out of going to church and I stayed home with dad. Unfortunately, I was a little young at the age of six to eight to get any great, wise conversation out of my dad and so I think I really did miss out on that learning period of father and son together. He died just before my ninth birthday on the 17th of May 1987. Strange as it might seem and very relevant when considering the latter years of my life, I do recall one conversation I had with my father. I must have been talking to dad about fighting and being strong. He was lying in bed, so he may have been sick with cancer by this stage, but he calmly said to me, "Eventually there's always going to be someone bigger and better at fighting". That was his statement. Nothing else except that. I don't know why I was interested in fighting back then, maybe it was what we were seeing on television, Fonzarelli in the Happy Days sitcom, or Magnum PI, or the movies on television, or perhaps it was because I was beginning to get into situations at school. Something though was happening at this early stage of life; maybe it was just me.

The doctors had given dad weeks or months if he was lucky, but he lasted a long time. Eventually he passed away and there were tears among the relatives and family. I was numb, and the gravity of the event seemingly didn't register with me. I remember feeling like something was wrong with me because I couldn't feel any pain from dad's passing. The reality is, it did affect me and as the years went by the devastating loss would become more and more evident. My brother, although visibly sad at the time, seemed to handle things better as time went by. He has always been that stable, sensible guy who went on to do some great things with his education and career. My sister survived the loss also, but mum was heartbroken. The love of her life taken from her at a relatively young age and now she was left with three small children to raise on her own. The times ahead would not be easy and certain events to come would almost bring us to the edge as a family. As far as mum could see, only by the grace of God would we make it through.

We were lucky in the early years while dad was still alive because, due to his income, we were able to attend private schools in Christchurch. By the time he passed on we were all attending Middleton Grange School in Riccarton, which was a Christian School. But this would become an expense our mother could no longer afford and so presumably at one stage

7

mum was going to have to pull us out of Middleton and send us to a public school. Fortunately though, there was a man on the school board who had sympathy with the family's situation and offered to pay our school fees from that moment on. In hindsight that was a really amazing gift of kindness and should have paved the way to success for the three of us. It certainly did for my brother and sister who remained at Middleton until their seventh and sixth form years. As for me, Middleton was a great building block, but the outdoors and physical activity had my attention, which made it difficult for me in the classroom. I really didn't see the importance of schooling and became easily distracted. There were certain subjects I did well at though: English, maths and physical education were all topics I was able to grasp easily. Due to my love of the outdoors and hunting I seemed to do well in English because I wanted to write stories like the books I was reading. But it wasn't enough really to hold my attention in the classroom and a few years before I left school, I started to seek out activities that involved being out of the classroom. One day when I was nine, we were at home in Rolleston, and I noticed a mob of sheep being driven past our front gate. It was a local farmer from not too far away shifting his flock from one place back to his home block. I walked down the driveway and hung over the steel gate and watched as this mob of a couple of hundred sheep went past followed by the farmer. As the last of them trailed by, the farmer and I locked eyes and he greeted me with a smile and a hello. The pair of us introduced ourselves and I was immediately interested in what he was doing and who he was. His name was Colin, he was about 177 cm tall, average build with a beard and balding on the top of his head because he was in his late forties. After exchanging words back and forwards we almost immediately became friends. For some reason mum came out to the end of the driveway and soon I had permission to follow along with Colin, thus beginning the friendship between him and I.

For the next year or so thereafter I would be ringing Colin to take me out on the farm. On my weekends away from school and our holidays I'd be out helping on the farm as much as I could which included shifting mobs of sheep, drenching sheep, doing the lambing beat in springtime and, of course, tailing the lambs at a later date. It seemed as though I had found a good person to spend some time with who would be able to teach me a few of the aspects of life a young lad needed to be taught at this young age. We were in the shearing shed crutching and shearing sheep, learning how to drive a tractor, shifting fences and learning some valuable life skills for the future. I had a passion for doing things that were considered manly; again I'm not sure where this came from, but I liked it. I wanted to be a man and a hunter and do the kinds of things that men would do. The rabbits and hares on Collin's farm soon became a target of my adventures. We would wait until darkness fell and then hunt using the headlights of the ute around the farm picking off the unsuspecting victims with a .22 calibre rifle. This was my first introduction to hunting and it was a fairly successful venture too as I became skilled with the workings of the rifle and the telescopic sights, hardly missing a shot and always coming back successful at the end of a hunt. Hunting definitely became an interest of mine, I started reading books about deer and learning about the wildlife we had in New Zealand which included the deer, wild pigs, thar, chamois and wild goats. There were also small numbers of wild sheep and cattle in different parts, but they were considered feral rather than wild like the deer and alpine animals. I was fascinated by them, developing a real love of the animals and the environment they lived in. Eventually I would read book after book on hunting which probably was the major contributor of my reading and writing skills in those younger years at least. Not everything I read was on hunting though. I did read a large number of the Willard Price adventures, as well, during a time when mum had experimented by removing the television from our house. Mum later commented on the huge difference it made having no television in the house. All of us children spent more time doing the more important activities that so often get misplaced when you're glued to the T.V.

Things continued to move along in the Donaldson household. Mum seemed to be doing okay, Beth was eleven and James was twelve by this time. James played a string instrument called the cello and did well at school. Beth loved horses, and I was the outdoors kid, working on the farm and playing sport. The New Zealand rugby team, the All Blacks, were on television even then and at some stage I took an interest in that also. Sport was my main activity at school too; out on the field at morning tea and lunchtime playing rugby and soccer with the other boys. School wasn't too bad in the early days, just learning slowly about the general challenges that life presents to us.

And then one day I was confronted by a challenge that would possibly mark a change in me that wouldn't be turned around for years to come. It was on the school bus which we caught from Rolleston to Christchurch every day. I was sitting on the bus which was packed full of children, my brother and sister were there, and we were halfway to town when one of the young Māori boys who caught the bus with us everyday day obviously noticed me sitting there silently. He was a child from the Burnham Military Base who would have been traveling into town for school, not the same school as us but obviously taking the same route as us to get to school. He came up to me and dangled a piece of paper in front of me that had something insulting written on it. I can't recall exactly what it was but I knew it to be offensive. I quickly grabbed the paper and scrunched it in defiance of whatever it was that was on the paper but within a split second a premeditated punch came precisely at the same time as the paper was grabbed. Because the paper was there, I couldn't even see it coming and it got me right in the face. Boom! Obviously this kid had thought that through and for whatever reason, decided that that was a good thing to do. I'd never been in a fight before where a punch was used and that really took me by surprise. I'd had wrestling fights before with my brother and probably friends at school but, as far as I can remember, that was the first time I'd had a serious strike in the face. Embarrassed and unsure of what to do I just sat there as the boy moved away through the crowd of people on the bus. And that was that; I'd just been taught a lesson about human nature. Talking with my mother and sister afterwards the question arose as to what I had done wrong which I was unaware of and so had no explanation for, but my sister had her own explanation. She said that it was probably because I was sitting there smiling constantly. I was afraid that she was correct, I didn't realise that I had been smiling but I was afraid that it was my lack of coolness that had been the cause of my own misfortune. Perhaps I thought, it was my fault. From then on, I would be more careful, I would try not to let something like that happen again. Unbeknown to me though it would be many years before I mastered the skill of not getting into fights; I had a long road in front of me and this was only the beginning.

CHAPTER 2

ONE ROAD

As time went by, I grew and developed into a keen young boy. More and more I was looking to be out doing the more adventurous activities. I had a few friends at school who were also interested in similar activities; the sport, the hunting and the outdoor activities. I was still working with Colin regularly and one of my relatives had come out with us a couple of times too. Colin to me was a good contact. I wasn't knowledgeable about the character of a person and right living back then. It never entered my mind the dangers that lay in wait for us in this big wide world. Colin was there to do the fun things with like farming and hunting and when he made some weird comments about my relative on a couple of different occasions it never even occurred to me that there was cause for concern. It never occurred to me that he was a bad guy. I was nine and my relative was eleven. Collin would let us sit in his lap and steer the ute while he was driving. At two different times he commented that he had a strange sensation when my relative was driving, and he asked her if she did also. In essence he was dirty. How I wish I was smarter and wiser back then at that young age, but I wasn't and so played out a scenario which would affect my relative probably for life. To this day I still regret what happened on this particular day. I know I was only nine, but I still look back and blame myself for not being tougher and smarter. After all Colin was my friend. In any case the incident happened, and I can't change that now. We are probably lucky it wasn't worse, but it was bad enough and I think the incident from that moment on changed my opinion of authority and adults. We couldn't trust them anymore and their lives were a sham. I'm assuming these are some of the underlying subconscious thoughts that prevailed thereafter. On this particular day Colin took us out swimming at the Waimakariri River and since we didn't have swimming togs, Colin decided we should go swimming without togs. He convinced my relative but not me. I had my shorts on, but my relative was naked and Colin, over the duration of an hour or so, took lots of photos of her in basically pornographic positions. He was also getting excited about it at the same time because I distinctly remember his body language or perhaps, functions might be more appropriate terminology. That was that - one bad guy. A loss of innocence for my relative and I, and an uncertain road ahead of us if you consider the potential damage an incident of this nature could have on two children at our stage of life.

Sometime during the weeks that followed my relative told my mum about what happened and a phone call was made to Colin to ask if the photos had been developed. Colin made up an excuse saying that there had been an error with the film and so he was unable to develop them. Mum knew my relative was telling the truth, but I don't know how far she went with her investigations and following up on the incident. As far as I know it wasn't for twenty years or more before the issue was raised with police. From that moment on though the relationship between our families was permanently destroyed and things would never be the same again. I really don't know the effects that my relative suffered because she is a strong person, but I'm very sure this was a negative experience for her and one that we all wish had never happened. It's just one of those things that you look back on in hindsight and you say that's never going to happen again. Not with my family anyway.

And so, we went forward again as a family and faced the same battles as we'd faced before. It was very difficult for my mother, and she really struggled with raising three children on her own. Money was hard to come by. Even though mum was receiving government support, the bills just became too much and it wasn't long before she decided we would have to sell our five-acre farm and move to town closer to school. I really didn't want to leave the countryside and I'm not sure how the others felt but there wasn't much we could do about it, we were going. The last day we were at Rolleston I climbed up onto the roof and wouldn't come down for half an hour or more, but I had no choice. Eventually I came down and got into the car as we all said goodbye to our family home. This was it; we were on our way to the city, and we were going to have to live with it.

We moved to Riccarton, onto Arthurs Street which happened to be five hundred metres down the road from the entrance to our school. Riccarton was okay as far as suburbs went, just an average suburban area in Christchurch City. There were some peaceful locations in the area, a couple of reasonable parks, some good schools and a mixture of low-cost housing through to the better areas where the more expensive properties were found. Further over towards Fendalton it was much nicer again but that was at least a ten-minute drive from our area. Arthurs Street was right in the middle as far as mum was concerned. We couldn't complain. Nearby Blenheim Road had industrial areas, and Church Corner and Riccarton Road were commercial areas. Generally speaking everything we really needed was within reach, so for mum I think it wasn't such a bad spot. The house on Arthurs Street consisted of weatherboard and an iron roof with a little brickwork inside and four main bedrooms. It was old, but still up to scratch for living in, and in hindsight we were probably lucky to have what we had.

During my time at Arthurs Street and Middleton Grange I grew in age and size to the point where I was a strong young guy. Some of us at the school were pretty tough kids and we played hard on the field to win every game we were involved in.

By the time I was twelve mum had paid for my membership to the New Zealand Deer Stalkers Association and through this association I developed my hunting skills and, of course, my physical ability. Club trips would happen on a monthly basis, and we'd all load up the club Land Rover and head off into the mountains in pursuit of big game and venison. By the time I was thirteen years old I had shot my first deer. I shot it on a trainee trip along the Townsend River which flows out into the Lees Valley. It was a very big deal at the time. From then on, I would continue to hunt nearly every weekend. If I wasn't out on a club trip, I'd be organising goat shooting trips with club guys for the weekends in-between the club trips. I must give credit to the guys I met through the Deer Stalkers Association and went hunting with. Most of them were pretty good guys. I wasn't a relative of theirs and they weren't obligated to take me out hunting, but they did, and we had some pretty awesome hunts too. Admittedly, I was the one finding properties on Banks Peninsula to hunt on and so that was a reason to take me out. There were other trips I was also invited on into areas I had no connection with, but I was still invited and well looked after, so those guys definitely deserve the credit for the way they spent time with me and helped me out. Some of the places we went were pretty extreme too, like the Dobson River down South, Glentanner, McCauley River, and South Westland. There were some scary and sometimes cold and isolated moments but in general we were fairly safe, and I learned some invaluable lessons that I wouldn't have gained had I not been through those experiences. Plus, it was great for health and strength building: carrying heavy packs up and down mountain sides, sleeping in huts and tents, and crossing rivers. Some of the hardest physical activity I've ever been involved with played out back then in the early days. Probably the hardest part would have been carrying those packs that literally felt like they were heavier than we were sometimes. That's when your body develops, that's when you learn how to push yourself. We shot a lot of animals too. Deer, chamois, thar, goats and pigs. Out of interest, the first real pig hunting I was involved with happened to be in Hanmer with friends of mums, rather than the Deer Stalkers Association. Nevertheless, they were all great times.

Some great people as well. I met a man called Neville Michington through the N.Z.D.A and spent a lot of time hunting with him. He was a well-loved Christian man who had his own children plus some foster children. If I'm correct, his children also went to Middleton Grange School at some stage. He was a good family man with a lovely wife, and it was quite sad when only a few years after I first met him, he drowned in the Ashley River. I shot a few deer with Neville and as I said we spent some good times out in the wilderness. Gordon Dennis was another good guy I met in my younger years. I actually met him for the first time on a school trip out to Glenroy, which is past Darfield heading towards the Alps. Gordon was hosting the group from my school on his farm while we stayed in the Baptist Camp in Glenroy. I made friends with Gordon straight away and some of the teachers suggested it would be a good idea for Gordon to spend some time with me considering the circumstances with my father passing and so forth. So, from then on and for some time afterwards Gordon and I made trips over to the West Coast where Gordon had another twelve-hundred-acre property which was in between the Hokitika River and the bush clad hills running up behind the Hokitika River. The farm was fairly wild country and we had to enter either by swing–bridge at the gorge, or by horseback across the Hokitika River further down where it was crossable. Over the course of the trips into the block we rode horses, trapped possums, shifted cattle and thoroughly enjoyed our time in there. I remember making cups of tea over a smoking fire and hunting along the riverbed, burning the tails off lambs at lambing time and the enjoyment of getting back to a pressure-cooked hot meal once we made it back across the river to Gordon's home away from home. Unforgettable times. Something can really be said about spending time in the wilderness and living that old lifestyle. I'd recommend it to anyone who has that opportunity.

Back in Christchurch my mother will tell you things were not going so well. Of course, my older brother James was doing really well, and Beth seemed to be doing okay, but in my case the people who knew me said that since my father had died, I had turned from a good kid quite quickly into a troubled child. The only time I seemed happy was when I was out hunting or on some mission out to the countryside. My moods weren't good, I hadn't picked up on the basic required routines of life, and they were correct in saying that I was troubled. I argued with my mother, stayed up late at night, and in school my relationships with other students began to fray. In fact, I began to fight. Kids at school knew I had a bad temper, and they would wind me up and pull at a few visible threads when opportunities presented themselves. Regrettably, it wasn't always one sided and I definitely knew how to pick on the people I didn't like. I made life difficult for a few people at school, so I was just as guilty as anybody else. But the scene was set early. I was struggling with the simple things, and from then on life got worse. I remember a couple of serious fights at school. One kid called James Sutherland, who was a year ahead of me and probably ten kilograms heavier than me, picked on me one time on the field. Even though I'd never trained to fight in any classes, by this stage I'd picked up grappling skills from wrestling and obviously gained a lot of strength from the outdoors which enabled be to do some unusual things. He was pushing into me and trying to dominate me, yelling and carrying on when I reached up and grabbed his hair on the top of his head. I wrenched his head down to waist height and then hit him about three times in the face before letting him go. He came up seeing a few stars I imagine and looked a bit lost as to where he was, but the fight stopped after that. He went off with a bleeding nose and a little confused as to how that had happened. That was the first time I think that I'd ever hit someone in the face in a serious fight other than wrestling. The next day one guy from his year came up to me and said he was stunned by what had happened and that he would never give me a hard time again. It's hard to forget those moments and, although the incident to most people would be a time you shouldn't want to remember, I felt good about it. I wasn't going to let anyone make a wimp out of me, never, that could never happen. That mind-set by now was stuck in my mind - if I was tough, I was okay.

I can't really remember all the fights from back then, but I know there were a few, mostly wrestling but bordering on serious sometimes. One time I was in Hanmer, I was still very young, possibly ten or eleven and I was waiting for my mother who was in some church meeting at a school. So, I was outside waiting around in the school yard and of course there were kids hanging around the same age as me. One was a big boy, bigger than me and as per usual we got into a fight. It went on for a while, I pinned him to the ground, and it basically ended on a good note as afterwards we started talking as friends, but somehow my mother had found out that we were fighting and later that day she got really angry with me and said to me, "I can't take you anywhere without you getting into a fight".

It's just a memory I know, but there was something in that statement which I haven't forgotten. From time-to-time memories pop up of things that went on back then and I know it was early days, but things were starting to happen back then. In the years to come, fighting would snowball into events I can't even legally write on paper. I had it in me, but for some reason to this day I can't forget all those times when I didn't initiate the fight. So many times, I was standing there doing nothing and was approached as a contender for a fight. People wanted to fight me; without a doubt people wanted to fight me. Later in life I would guarantee to you that it was my looks, it was my baby face that led to the fights and that people were just starting the fights because they thought I wasn't able to hold my ground and therefore I wouldn't be confident. The numbers of fights were countless as I grew older, and I knew I wasn't the one starting most of them. The reality is that so many of the fights I ever became involved with were straight out self-defence. But again, this is human nature, and a lot of the time people aren't very nice. You must learn to deal with this, and you deal with it as best as you know how. I only knew one way. I was on one road, a road that started off with aggression and violence and would lead me through a world of alcohol, drugs and gang life. This was the beginning.

As time went by, friends began to change, and life began to change. My mother sent me to Blenheim for six months to stay with a Christian family up there who owned a farm. I went to Marlborough Boys College during the time that I was there. While at Marlborough Boys College I was introduced for the first time to the phenomenon of the "Home Boys" and the "White Boys". Not surprisingly the "Home Boys" had a much larger gathering, largely due to the latest trends and pop culture that was being displayed on televisions and radios throughout the country. In fact, the Home Boys' music was just taking off in the form of rap or gangster music. It was visibly obvious throughout the school and beyond that this gangster culture was going to be a big thing. Baggy clothes, the haircuts, the shoes, and the language. White kids and Māori boys made up the numbers of the Home Boys, there were lots of them and they were definitely the more popular culture among the youngsters during that time. The "White Boys" were much fewer in number. Called the White Boys by name, but from my experience firstly in Blenheim and later in life, it was always a mixed bunch. Nearly every group I've known labelled as White Boys always had Māori boys hanging out with them. Such was the case in Blenheim, there were half a dozen guys there known as the White Boys and among them were three big Māori. So, it wasn't so much of a group of Europeans, as a group not going along with everyone else. These guys didn't embrace the modern-day rap culture that was sweeping the country and had taken on more of a European bad boy approach to life. Metallica music, short hair and scruffy clothes. These were the guys I spent my lunch times with. But it was a relatively short period and not a lot was achieved in that time unfortunately. From my mother's perspective I certainly didn't make any progress. I had a few fights that I remember, lifting one guy over a balcony at school which left him hanging on by his fingertips. He was the one who decided he had a problem with me, I don't recall any real lead up to it, so I don't know why, it just happened. There was another scuffle on the front field too with about three or four people but it didn't get very far after being broken up by a senior student.

Fights and the new life experience aside, it was over before it began and within six months I was heading back to Christchurch. Back in Christchurch I reconnected with some of my old friends. These guys were getting into some new things. At that young age of thirteen to fourteen I began experimenting with alcohol, cigarettes and of course marijuana. I still had a few months left at school before I was out on my own recognisance and so it started shortly after I returned to Christchurch. I endured my last few months at a different high school than the one I'd previously attended. This time it was Lincoln High School on the edges of town where I think mum hoped I would encounter some of the farming community. Unfortunately, that was not the case and, yet again, I spent the next few months getting myself into trouble and getting into fights. By the time I fell out with the Senior Principle at Lincoln, I think everyone knew that my school days were over. It was a bit of a shame, there had been some potential as I grew up, but it just had not come to fruition. One of my greater achievements was playing rugby. I'd actually made it into the Canterbury School Boys' rep team and played in a tournament down south in Dunedin. I was in the under forty-five-kilogram team so admittedly it was when I was fairly young but it's just a shame I never followed through on it. It could have been a good thing. The hope was that while at Lincoln, I would find myself and move into the farming sector. Having previously shown a lot of interest in this area, they thought that this was the best option for me. I don't think anyone really knew that deep down I was not a happy guy; I was angry, missing my dad who'd been gone for a few years now, and obviously a little mixed up over certain things that had taken place. Parts of life I just didn't understand, things were missing, and things were not good. I found myself struggling to get through the challenges I was facing. Not knowing who to turn to or what to do I found myself indulging in cigarettes and alcohol on a regular basis. It was an escape for me and for some reason those cigarettes did seem to have a calming effect. That's what I thought anyway.

My friend and I were fourteen and had just been at a concert in Hagley Park in Christchurch City. We were half drunk and walking back down Riccarton Road, one of the main roads running through my area. It was night-time, yet the street was busy with traffic and pedestrians. In a moment's time I was about to be introduced to my new world. It was just minutes away. Standing on the corner of Rotherham Street and Riccarton Road was a guy I would soon become familiar with, a guy that would introduce me to this new world. Black jeans, black jersey, steel cap boots and a bald head with a small moustache. His name was Matlock, and we were about to become well acquainted with him. Donnacha, my Irish friend, and I approached the street corner where Matlock was standing and thus began our conversation.

Matlock: "How's it going guys?"

"Good", was my reply. That was my usual reply to most greetings.

"Where are you guys heading? You guys want to come to a party?" Matlock asked.

Slightly intoxicated himself, Matlock seemed to take an immediate liking to us. Because of our looks and dress Matlock must have assumed we were young White Boys hence the overly friendly communication. We exchanged names and I curiously asked what the party was about. Matlock continued, "Down at the clubhouse, you know the one?"

"Yep, I know the one," I replied as I pointed in the direction of the corner of Rotherham and Peverel where the heavily fortified double storied gang pad sat.

"You know who it is in there, guys?" Matlock asked. I gave him the wrong answer thinking that it was a different Christchurch club. Matlock fired back, "Na mate there aren't no scumbags like that in here". Even after giving the wrong answer, Matlock wasn't fazed. "Only the good guys in there boys, only the good guys".

So, we were invited and we followed along, not afraid but just looking for an adventure, looking for some excitement in this town of ours. It was only a short walk from the corner of Riccarton Road to the other end where the clubhouse stood. I'd been passed it before and seen from the outside, but never had I walked through those gates. From the outside you could see a very large double-storied house surrounded by an eight-foot, corrugated iron fence with barbed wire on top and heavy steel gates at the front. A big, old willow tree stretched up into the sky and dangled its branches down over the fence. If you looked up into the top storey window of the old house you could see gang paraphernalia clearly pinned up against the window frame. The paint was fading, and you could tell by looking at it that this place was a lair, a hangout. I learned in the years to follow that the clubhouse was an old monastery, which is why it had a fairly awesome look about it. The house was big and old. As we neared the clubhouse the sound of old-school music travelled out onto the street and Matlock, reaching the gate, rang the buzzer for us. We heard keys and then the big steel gate began to open, and we were on our way into one of New Zealand's notorious underworld clubs for the first time.

There was a party going on inside as we neared the building. Donnacha and I had no idea what we were walking into, but we were relaxed and still a bit intoxicated which probably helped with the situation. Outside the house, guys in their thirties and forties leaned against the house and stood on the steps. A lot of black jerseys, black jeans, leather boots and leather jackets. The guy who first opened the gate for us was a big guy too, about six foot three inches and well-built with a bald head. He was wearing the club patch on his back which happened to be the first time I'd ever seen it. As we walked in, we were introduced to him. Over the years to follow this guy became a close friend of mine and we ended up spending a lot of time together but for his personal privacy I'll leave his name out of the pages of this book. I'll call him Uncle. Uncle had a few tattoos but one of his most distinguishing features was his long face and nose, everybody who knew him will know what I'm talking about. Looking around the rest of the yard as I walked in, I saw a few bald heads, a few "long hair" heads and a lot of facial hair. These guys were bikers, and there was a lot of them. We walked through the old monastery front doors with the stained-glass surrounds and into the downstairs bar. I was in the middle of the biker lair. Black walls, bar, bar tables, stairs leading up, a stage, swastikas on the walls, a lot of smoke, guys playing cards at the tables, loud music and an atmosphere that I've never really come across since. I've been to several different clubhouses over the years, but none were like this. It also had a lot to do with the people, these guys were straight out of the seventies. Old school, staunch bikers. Most of the guys were wearing a patch, and it was also painted above the stage and on various memorabilia around the house. I knew where I was straight away and for some reason, I didn't mind it. For now, it was a good place to be. I had a sense that I was surrounded by people who were safe for me to be around, I don't know why but for some reason I didn't think this was a dangerous place. Probably because of my age too, obviously, I mean why would these guys want to give me a hard time? I was lucky if I was half their age.

Donnacha and I left later that night and headed back to our separate family homes. Smelling of smoke and beer I'm pretty sure we both got in trouble for that late night out, but for me there wasn't a lot my mother was able to do. Just grateful I was home, I guess. As for Donnacha I'm not sure if that was his first and only time he came to the club or if he came back with me maybe one more time, but I do know that at some stage his parents got wind of what we were up to, and I didn't really see him a lot after that. In fact, it was probably one of the last times I did see Donnacha, which was a shame because he was a good guy and we'd done a bit of hunting and exploring together on a number of different occasions. But that's the way things go.

As for me I was keen to return there to the clubhouse and hangout. I liked the idea of a place where you could have a drink and a smoke and be around some older guys who knew how to look after themselves. To all intents and purposes, they knew how to stand their ground in their own territory. They were obviously a bit of an army of their own and I'd never come across people like that before. After all the trouble I had had over the years, maybe I thought, this was a good thing for me.

CHAPTER 3

THE CLUB

Days can really drag when you're young and don't have much to get on with. That was me at the time, a little bored and looking for some excitement. I spent a bit of time with my old friends, we'd hang out and have a few drinks and the odd smoke, but really I wanted to head back down to the club and see what I could get myself into. So that's what I did. After a couple more visits to the club, Uncle and I quickly became friends. Uncle at the time was about twenty-eight years old so in reality he became more of an older brother than a friend. But over the weeks to follow I got to know him and his lovely girlfriend Shell. Shell was beautiful I thought, late twenties as well, a small and petite woman with straight blond hair that went halfway down her back. And she was a good sort too. But we all got along anyway, and I looked up to Uncle a lot. During my first few weeks hanging out at the club I met a number of the different members and got an idea of what was going on there. During the week it was a bit quieter with a handful of people coming and going but one hundred percent of the time there was always someone there watching the pad and keeping an eye on the gate and security. Uncle began to talk to me about certain things, just basic stuff, but I was learning a bit here and there. I didn't have to learn to keep my mouth shut though. I was good at that already. These guys were pretty serious, and I don't reckon I would have been there long if I'd started being loud. Most of these guys were white with the exception of one member who was a Māori. There were Māori woman who were either married to members or girlfriends of members and there were also Māori supporters who would visit, so this was by no means a racist club, but it was predominantly European. I guess that I was comfortable with that because that's who I was and that's who I'd grown up with. The other factor which would have played a part was the fact that a number of the people I had experienced aggression from as I was growing up were either Māori or Pacific Island people and, they had tended to have their own kind of gangs, so to me this appeared to be basically a gang for guys like me or so I thought. I must make a distinction though fairly quickly, that back in those days the word gang was never used. In fact, "gang" was a bad word. The club only ever described itself as a motorcycle club. It was a patch wearing motorcycle club and, in those days, there was seen to be a fairly major difference between the Māori and Polynesian patch wearing gangs and the often-European patch wearing motorcycle clubs. I guess things were probably different in other parts of the country. For Christchurch and the South Island, you tended to see more of the European guys in the bike clubs and other guys joining the non-bike clubs. The motorcycle clubs were known to be fairly well organised, more of a middle-class, blue-collar type of environment and you could attribute certain qualities to these clubs that other groups like the street gangs, for example, seemed to be lacking. Secrecy for one thing, a lot more exclusive and definitely harder to join. Which brings me to my strange appearance on the scene back in those days when a motorcycle club was definitely not the place for a young teenager to be hanging out. Why was I even allowed in there?

The guys liked me; they thought I was a good young fella. I hadn't really seen any other young people there apart from myself and my mate

Donnacha. The next youngest I'd seen were the likes of Matlock in his early twenties and a few other guys I'd become friends with. Out of all the members Uncle was the youngest at the age of twenty-eight. There was an idea that it wasn't a bad thing to have the odd young guy hanging around so you can get them learning the ropes from a young age, but by no means was it anything like the street gangs where they had a lot of young people hanging around trying to get in. It just wasn't like that. Most of the guys I knew at the club were men and it was an adult environment. I guess the reason I was there was because I just started coming around and I was persistent and eventually my face was accepted. But that acceptance wouldn't come immediately. There were times I was told to come back at a different time, and it was definitely a gradual thing. To slow that process down a little was the plan for me to go down south and do the agricultural course. And that's what I ended up doing. I would have been getting through my fourteenth year or close to fifteen when I went down south to Balclutha for a four-month farming course.

Whilst in the south I spent some time with my real uncle, my mum's brother, attended the course and spent over twenty-one weeks working on two different farms down there. It was worth while doing and I added to my already reasonably strong outdoorsy and farming background, but I did not complete the paperwork for the course, only the practical side which consisted of the twenty-one weeks on the farms. It would have been nice to get the paperwork along with the experience, but I wasn't too worried about the qualification and so started making plans for what was to come next. To add to that, while I had been down there I still really wasn't in the right frame of mind. I kept thinking about Christchurch. I guess I missed my family and friends and, of course, I still had this issue of liking the drink and the marijuana. Had the latter not been a part of the equation I may have walked away from the south with the qualification. But nevertheless,

I was fairly adamant that I wanted to be heading back to Christchurch and that's just what ended up happening.

Back in Christchurch I found myself drawn to the same activities as before I left. I was back at the club almost straight away. By this stage I was starting to think that this is who I wanted to be. To me these guys had things sussed. They had the bikes, great bikes, mostly Triumph and Harley Davidson but there were Italian bikes as well and basically as long as it was British, American or European it was accepted. And it wasn't just the bikes the members had either, they all had great woman, they were tough guys too. Mean looking, and you just knew that these guys were dangerous and together as a force they were strong. The fact is that this particular club was known right throughout New Zealand. They were known as a force you didn't want to cross. As far as Christchurch was concerned, they were the leading club or gang in the city. They were the men. None of the other gangs really wanted to have any problem with them. Of course, it wasn't always peaceful and things did go on, but I know for a fact that this club, the one that I was slowly being accepted into, was one of the most feared in the country. So as I said, these guys had a life that I was beginning to admire more and more. I wanted this and although it's often hard to picture yourself as an older person when you're young I thought that if I did get old, I wanted to be one of these guys.

By this time, I was fifteen years old, and I was basically going to the club every night of the week and getting on the alcohol and of course having the smokes and crashing out there most nights. Some of the older guys were hesitant to have such a young guy around and words were spoken among members along the lines of "This place isn't no orphanage". There was the possibility that my access to the club would be hindered, but due to some of the guys I had connected well with the issues were resolved and it was agreed that I could live there, much to my surprise. I was going to be allowed to pay just twenty bucks a week and I could live there, but it came with a clause. I would be given duties and basically I would be doing chores around the pad and cleaning up as a way of contributing to my rent. If I could do a good job, it would work out in everyone's favour. I agreed and not long after I moved into the clubhouse where I was given my own room and a key and access to the house and basically everything. I was set, or so I thought. Basically, I was the lowest form of life on the food chain within the hierarchy, but I didn't care, I was a part of the group and that's all I wanted at this stage. I was just happy to be involved.

As time went by, I was getting schooled on a lot of different things. Uncle and I would spend a fair bit of time together and I was a fast learner. By this stage there was more than just one uncle. Now I had a whole army of uncles around me. I don't really want to use names for most of the members and main people for this book on my life because it's just not necessary and most of these guys are still alive to this day, but I can give my own nicknames to them for the sake of this story. Just thinking about it all now just brings back so many memories and faces. I know them all. Lot of members too, the ones close to me in the beginning were a lot of the younger members but then, as I got older, I started to get along better and better with the older members too.

The days for a while consisted of drinking whisky during the day, smoking pot, going for rides on the bikes, parties during the weekends, and numerous other activities. I didn't yet have my own bike, but I was saving at the time and, surprisingly, that money built up fast. I got my money from the government in those early days, it was called a Youth Payment. This benefit gave me a hundred odd dollars per week to survive on. It wasn't a lot, but I still managed to survive and pay the rent and save. Admittedly, and to the amusement of those who knew me, my mother would often bring clean washing and food to the pad gate for me. That helped out a lot too. Goodness knows how hard it was for my mother at the time, but I guess she coped, and rightly so because at least I was with adults. In a way I was a lot safer there than I could have been in a lot of other possible situations. Back then, and equally so now, there were a lot of bad, bad scenes people could find themselves mixed up with. There was the junky scene and that was really bad. People would be overdosing and basically killing themselves on heroin. Then there was the street gang scene with the Black Power and the Mongrel Mob. I don't want to go into details, but that was not a safe scene for a guy like me especially at that age. There was the Home Boys and the Skin Heads and the Punks and numerous other factions and groups around town. It was really so easy to get swamped in those bad scenes where some people never came out. At least where I was the guys were a lot more level-headed. They knew how to avoid interaction with police and those undesirable scenes where the bad stuff was going on. As far as being involved with the underworld went, if you had to be involved then this club I was with wasn't a bad option. Yes, there was alcohol, drug use from time to time, violence and the potential for inter-gang violence, but really the group I was a part of had been around for a long time and they were experienced, they knew how to remain low key and avoid bad circumstances. Plus, there were rules. Part of what I was getting schooled on was the rules of what you could and couldn't do as a member or associate of the club. You could not use drugs or needles which were deemed as junky substances and techniques. You could not drink and drive as a member or prospect. You could not ever give a statement to police, never. Don't say anything, just ask for a lawyer. You could not pass on club secrets or sensitive information to anybody which included things like names and numbers of members and associates. There was also an unwritten code of conduct which was self-explanatory; if you behave like a dick and people don't like you then obviously things are not going to work out well for you and in some cases, things worked out very badly for individuals. I guess in a way this is why some of us were safe here, but other people were safe in other places. Maybe if you weren't the right type of person then you would have been better off hanging out with the punks or the skins or the Home Boys. My reason for that is, if you could stick to the rules, you would be okay but if you were bad at breaking the rules then you might be better off in an environment which is less structured and organised. Meaning less rules made it easier for people to not break the rules. I guess that's where it gets a little confusing for some people. Don't worry I wasn't perfect, and I definitely broke the odd rule but generally speaking I knew how to keep myself alive and that to me was simple. Don't mess up with these guys.

CHAPTER 4

THROUGH THE EYES
AND THE EARS

They say that through the eyes and ears is how a child learns and what came through my eyes and ears would shape me in a fairly unique way. I had a good memory for basically everything, I can remember conversations sometimes that I've had twenty-five years ago depending on the importance of the content. With regards to what I learnt in those years of my mid to late teens when I was doing a lot more listening than talking, I picked up on a lot of things and I certainly saw a lot.

One time I was sitting in the bar area with a prospect who later became a member, I'll call him Miller. This guy is not one you'd forget easily, he loved the club, loved bikes and he loved being a biker. Miller, who was of a solid build would have looked intimidating enough to the general public. He had broad shoulders, big arms and legs, shaved head with tattoos and a long mullet coming out the back. Miller always wore basically the same style every time you saw him: black denim jeans, black tee-shirts, steel cap boots and black jerseys. Only his half jacket with the club prospect rocker on it wasn't black, the half jacket was a heavy blue denim jacket. The half jacket, which is often also referred to as a vest, was basically a denim or

32

leather jacket without the sleeves. That is what the club patch went on and then that would be worn over the top of whatever else you were wearing, so basically the club patch and colours could be seen while you were socialising or riding your bike down the road. The club patch was the most prized possession. When I first met Miller he was only a prospect, so at that early stage he didn't have his patch. The prospects only had the bottom strip (known as the rocker) of the patch until they had done their full time and then they would be rewarded with the full patch

The full patch is made up of three pieces, the top rocker, the centre patch and the bottom rocker. This is a lot like most gang patches although there is one difference for motorcycle clubs. Beside the centre patch in a motorcycle club patch is a little square with the letters MC which stands for motorcycle club. So, the top rocker holds the name of the club, then the centre patch has the symbol of the club and then the bottom rocker has the name of the place the club is from so for this club the bottom rocker had the place name 'Christchurch' in the bottom rocker. The club at one stage also had a chapter in Dunedin but, by my time the Dunedin chapter had been closed down. Now, in the centre patch was the club symbol, but I can't reveal the symbol without revealing the club identity, so for now I can just say that it was probably one of the most offensive club centre patches I have ever seen. No other club in the history of New Zealand or the world for that matter had a club centre patch, some might say, that was quite as evil as the centre patch that The Club had in their patch. All I can say is that it contained symbolism that stood for death. It was evil.

Miller was doing his best to get his patch. He was prospecting and basically doing what he was told to achieve that result: he loved it too. But not only was it the patch that he loved, he also loved the acceptance to a clan, a brotherhood, a brotherhood that very few other people would ever be able to get into. Miller knew what this club would mean for his future and that's the future he wanted.

So, there was Miller and I leaning against the bar in the clubhouse, and we were discussing how things went with regards to problems with other people. Miller said to me, "If you have crap with any one or any group like the Road Knights for example, we'll back you up, because you're one of us now, we'll back you up".

I definitely liked the sound of it; this meant I had support. More importantly it also meant that I'd already been accepted, and I hadn't even started prospecting yet. This was highly unusual, such a young guy like myself being allowed to enter the circle. This was a big deal and after thinking about it I realised the fruits of that benefit were actually happening already. For example, one time when I was leaving Uncle's out in Hornby after a daytime visit, I was waiting for a ride on the corner of Uncle's street. I'd only been outside a few minutes and a few young Home Boys from the neighbourhood started hanging around on the other side of the road. Then they started looking over at me and exchanging comments among themselves, obviously not knowing that I had come out of Uncle's property. The atmosphere almost immediately turned a little cold, and I could tell something was up. They could see that I was a white boy and obviously they didn't like it. One of them muttered something across the street at me and although I couldn't make out what he'd said I knew it was something anti, so I calmly turned around and started walking away. I didn't bother looking back at them because I knew it was only moments away from something going down and I was easily outnumbered. All I could do was move away without looking like I was in a hurry and head back up Uncle's driveway and into his house. I walked back through the front door and quickly relayed to Uncle what had happened. "Hey man, I was just waiting out on the road and there's a group of Home Boys out there looking like they want a fight. One of them called something out across the road at me so I just walked back in here"

"Is that right?" Uncle replied. "Might have to give these pricks a hurry up," He continued, "Shall we give them a bit of a fright, ay?" Two seconds later the manhole in the roof was being removed and Uncle was up there before I had a chance to say anything with his legs dangling down through the hole. "Pass me that flashlight Shell" Uncle bellowed down from above. Seconds later and after a bit of thumping around Uncle dropped back out of the ceiling holding something wrapped in a cloth. The cloth came off and underneath was a sawn-off shotgun. Obviously, guns were nothing new to me, but this one in particular was a sawn off which means it is designed for being concealed, and for one other thing which is plainly obvious, shooting people at close range. A few more words were exchanged before Uncle and I jumped in the Valiant and reversed out his driveway. He was driving and I was in the passenger side. We rolled out onto the road anticipating some immediate confrontation and idled across the road heading towards the side the boys had been hanging around on. They were gone, not surprisingly, even though we'd only taken a couple of minutes to get out there, but the likelihood is they saw me heading up Uncle's driveway and decided to gap it. We continued to idle down the street and were about to turn left to head around the block when we spotted one walking away down the street. I'm not exactly sure if he was one of them but he fit the profile, so we pulled up right beside him and Uncle raised the sawn-off shotgun above the open glass of the passenger door by leaning across in front of me. All this young guy would have seen was two barrels pointing straight at him out of a Valiant and a couple of white guys, one of them heavily tattooed behind the wheel with his finger on the trigger like he was ready to pull it.

Nothing was said, just the eye contact and I suppose the warning look which was as if to say, "Watch it mate". The young guy knew and that was all Uncle's intentions were. We drove off again and drove around the block a couple of times before heading back to his place.

Rick was another good mate of mine. I first met Rick at the club, he rode in on his old-school Triumph Bonneville. He was actually a Timaru guy, but he'd recently moved to Christchurch and had wanted to connect with the club which he'd known about for some time. He ended up at the club house anyway, and knew Uncle and a few of the other guys. Rick was a big boy, in his thirties at the time. He was a big, tall, solid guy with a bald head and Roman nose. This guy genuinely looked like an oversized white boy, but he was on a Triumph, and he had an enthusiasm about bikes, so I guess he'd fit into the biker category. Good sort anyway, well at least he always was to me. I was at the club for a while before Rick came along, so I was already one of the "family," when Rick turned up. But for whatever reason Rick and I got on pretty well even though I was considerably younger than him. We were like good mates from the time we first met. He was another one along with Uncle who came into bat for me during those early days when I first started heading down to the club. There were these guys who had tried to give me a bit of a hard time on one particular occasion, so Rick and I found out where one of them lived and headed around. We'd only walked about a few metres up the guy's driveway and he was leaping over the fence and running to get away from us. I could hardly believe it. Something was going on here, these guys who in the past would have, without even thinking about it, started a fight with me were now running scared. Yes, it's true I had a couple of big ugly sidekicks who were making them scared, but it felt good. Felt like I was finally getting some justice in my life. I couldn't see a problem with this at all. This kind of incident over time would become child's play in comparison to what we'd get into in the future, but it was a teaser. It was enough to get me hooked on the buzz; the buzz of being in control.

I was taught the importance of being staunch early on. "Never back down, always stand your ground." The words rang through my ears. "I tell you mate", Uncle emphasised to me "One time we had those Nomads up North surrounding us and one of them come up to us with a shotty under a magazine and pointed it right at me. We were surrounded and there were only two of us and I just looked at him and said, 'Do it, pull it'. And that was that, they just sniggered at us and then walked off".

I was struggling to imagine myself in this position and was grappling with the idea of how do you always back it up? I wasn't sure but the words were going into my head and somehow, they were starting to stick. I also saw these guy's movements and their body language. You got an idea of what they were thinking from firstly what they were telling me but also how they were behaving. Over the years the body language was not so easy for me to become fluent in; perhaps this had contributed to the numerous fights I'd been involved with. But in any case, there came a time where I seriously overcompensated my lack of confident body language with a competence for violence. Truth be known I think I listened too well and all I had in my head was that you never back down, "Never let them beat you", and that "We are the best, we are the staunchest of the staunch. No one can mess with us and get away with it". That's what I was told. "This club is the staunchest club around and these members are the elite. The Crème de la Crème, the best of the very best." So, in spite of the fact that I was lacking in some kind of inner security, at the same time I was also overconfident in the fact that I believed we were unbeatable. I think I neglected some areas of personal development and focused almost too much on the need to win. I know for a fact I thought it was more important to be staunch (a capable fighter), than it was to have social skills.

The parties in those days were pretty full on. I remember bourbon nights at the club would be fully packed out with members and supporters.

Bourbon night was a Friday night and there were hundreds of litres of bourbon plus mix flowing. Alcohol was a big thing in those days, everybody drank alcohol, not everyone did drugs, but everybody did alcohol. By this stage I'd met a few girls my age and they would all come around on the weekends and get heavily intoxicated with us. I've always had a big thing for woman, and I was certainly no different back then so the woman were a big part of my life as well. All of them were unique in their own ways, there were a few bad ones of course but I still have fond memories of many. And what was a party without members of the opposite sex? Sometimes they were the life of the party.

There were also other clubs around that were basically friendly with our club. Clubs like the Devils Henchmen who were based in Christchurch and Timaru. The Mothers from Palmerston North, The Tyrants from Levin, the Confederates from Pahiatua and a few smaller side-patch clubs like Central MC from Taupo and the Plimmerton Boys from Plimmerton. All these clubs were on a friendly basis with each other and often parties would include these visitors from out of town or occasionally a few of the Christchurch Henchmen. Bikes, rides and parties were all that life revolved around for some, but without a doubt motorbikes were the central focus for everyone involved. Bikes were key. The first few rides I went on were a real buzz and an eye opener. One of the first rides I went on I recall phoning my mum and informing her about what I was doing. This was before I moved into the clubhouse. I said, "Mum I'm going on a club ride, it's a funeral". She was immediately concerned because she assumed that gang funerals were where problems occurred, and she imagined us being caught up in some sort of crossfire. But it wasn't like that at all. Uncle had a Triumph Trident with long and high T bars. The bars definitely suited the bike and topping it off were the extremely loud exhaust pipes that you could hear coming from kilometres away. Since I still didn't have a bike, I jumped on the back of Uncle's Trident and a group of about ten of us headed out from the club house and out to the funeral. It was a real buzz in those early years with a medium to large pack of bikes on the road. Cars knew who you were as soon as they saw you or heard you coming. Cars would pull over and let you past. People would nervously look straight ahead as you idled up beside them at lights, and kids would block their ears as the pack went past because the noise was so great.

Not long after I moved into the clubhouse I was invited on a ride and there were about seventy patched members in the ride on that occasion. Members included guys from the Riccarton club, and the Christchurch and Timaru Devils Henchmen. That was probably one of the better rides I went on and we ended up going right through the middle of Christchurch city centre. There would have been about seventy patch members on bikes plus supporters, so you can imagine the number of loud bikes on the road. There were bikes everywhere. It was literally so loud that the people standing on the side of the road watching were all blocking their ears at once to dull the noise. Streams of bikes were all over the road weaving in and out of traffic, overtaking and literally engulfing everything on the road in front of them. No police, nothing stopping us, and really a scene that you seldom see these days.

In those days some of the clubs were big, a lot bigger than they are now. The club I was involved with wasn't really big in numbers compared to some clubs, but it was feared based on its reputation. The Henchmen though were really big at this particular time so when they all came out on a ride with you it definitely enlarged the pack considerably. Another big ride I went on soon after moving into the club house was down to the Ashburton bike show. That particular time I recall there were so many it just wasn't funny. All our club, Christchurch and Timaru Henchmen, Tyrants, and numerous others were present in a line of bikes that stretched for hundreds of metres if not kilometres if you included all the stragglers. At that same bike show other clubs also showed up who were not necessarily on the same friendly basis. Road Nights were there, and also the Tribesman and Highway 61 had arrived together. There were a lot of them too. For me, still a kid and new to most of it, this was all pretty exciting stuff, and I was learning a lot. Just listening and watching. Taking it all in.

Obviously not everything I saw or heard was going to be good for me in the long run though, and experiences would come and go during those first few years that would change me forever. Some good, some bad. At this stage though it was important for me to remain close to the members and cement my place among them. I realised that survival depended on the club approving of me and allowing me to remain within the community. I did see things happen that would seriously put into question anybody's permanent position among the community, and I had heard stories of things that had happened to people who didn't make it. Not necessarily members who had fallen away but more supporters or prospects. Prospecting was an uncertain time for many because there was no guarantee that anyone would make it. One incident that immediately springs to mind was the time where big Rick's friend came unstuck with the members. Apparently, he had been at one of the Christchurch tattoo shops where the owner of the shop was friends with some of the club's members. So, John Dog had been getting a tattoo done and while he was in there he'd been talking away before the topic of our club came up. To cut a long story short, John basically told this guy he was prospecting for our club already but he wasn't, he was just a supporter at this time. Not long after John came around to the club house on a bourbon night expecting to get back on the drinks as he'd done previously. Unfortunately for him though it wasn't going to be the same as every other time and within a few minutes he was asked outside to talk to one of the members. I'll call the member Dougal for the purpose of this story. Dougal had a problem with John's false claim. Whether or not that problem was of concern to other members as well, which it probably was, I don't know but it was obviously a big enough problem that it was going to be taken care of on that night and not the way John wished. Dougal walked him around the back of the pad, knocked him over and let him fall up against the dog cage where the club dog named Hellhound grabbed him through the bars and tore away at his calf muscle. That went on for a few minutes and then he was booted out the front gate and sent away. I didn't actually see this happen, but I got told about it straight after.

Then there was another incident which I did see. One of the prospects, who had only been prospecting a short while but who had known some of the members for a long time, was drinking up at the bar. According to the members, the prospect whose name was Shorty had been sitting there getting more and more drunk as the night went on. I was watching from the other side of the bar but didn't hear the conversation. One of the members had been reminiscing about some times gone past and Shorty, who was not very familiar with this member, had in a bit of a drunken haze questioned this member's memory on one of the topics. Next thing I remember was looking across seeing Shorty flat on the ground after having a full-size bar stool smashed across the back of his head. He was completely out to it, unconscious. I just remember looking at him and feeling a bit bad because he was one of us. He was like a brother already even though he hadn't been there very long and here he was knocked out on the floor, and no one was helping him. But that's the life though, that's the way it was. We saw him just a couple of days later and it was like nothing had happened. So yes, he recovered but it was a warning to him and the rest of us too. The reality is this was no kindergarten and if I wasn't careful that would happen to me too. Shorty carried on after that prospecting for a while. He wasn't a bad guy Shorty; I remember him well even though it's been quite a few years since I've seen him. And yes, he had that nickname for a reason. The classic joke whenever Shorty was around was whether or not he wanted a box to stand on when he was up at the bar. Shorty also had a Triumph Trident, and he was fast on his way to making his way in the club life before another more serious event happened to him that pretty much put him out permanently. Shorty was on Dougal's Harley Davidson Sportster one day and he was passing a car on the right-hand side when the car decided to turn right into a side street and wiped out Shorty. You would think Shorty might have seen that coming but obviously not, perhaps he'd been drinking. Anyway, Shorty ended up with broken hips and legs and for a long time after that we didn't see him. One thing I know for sure is that was the end of his prospecting.

CHAPTER 5

TROUBLE BREWING

My mother raised us to believe in a higher power. God. At the Christian school where we went there was a general understanding among everyone that God was real. Jesus Christ was the son of God and the saviour of mankind. At church on Sunday everybody believed. My Aunty (dads' sister) and Uncle from up North believed and had been missionaries in Spain for a long time. All our family on my mother's side was grounded in the Christian faith to varying degrees. To me it had been a part of life and even though I obviously was not living the Christian way at this present point in time, I still had these early teachings well entrenched in my mind. I remember being by myself upstairs at the clubhouse one time and thinking about God and at that moment I surmised that maybe I do believe. From memory I think I was afraid that it might be real and therefor hell would be real also. I reasoned that I must not disregard the faith, so that if it does indeed turn out to be real, I would not be disqualified. Immediately I concluded that this should never, ever be revealed under any circumstances to anyone in my club life. I knew without a doubt that this revelation would destroy my reputation and any future I might have within this circle. I had to maintain the stance that I was the same as them. Any mention of the Christian faith would highly likely be viewed as a sign of weakness or instability of the mind. They may well have already known my previous background but because of the way I was around them they must have assumed that I was not a believer. I seem to recall the faith being mentioned at some stage possibly when we were drinking and getting intoxicated one night and the immediate response from Uncle gave the direct indication that this was not something to be mentioned under any circumstances. The top man, the president, would shut any such talk down very quickly, and knowing now what I know everybody else was leaning in the same direction. Whether or not anybody else had any thoughts along faith-based lines at any time I cannot confirm; thoughts probably entered their minds from time to time just like any normal person but one thing I know for sure is even if you had those thoughts, you would never mention it because it simply was not cool. You could say it was unacceptable behaviour or, like politics, just something that you never mentioned.

Having decided at that stage that I should not disregard the faith, I think it would be fair to say that the upbringing I had received held truly little other hold over me. I was doing everything else I wanted to do any time or day of the year. There were no rules other than the rules of the club and by no means was I living a moral life. Perhaps with the inclination that as I was still a child or youth I would not be held accountable, I simply went about my life with little or no concern for the spiritual world. Most definitely I believe that the older I got the less I would have thought about such things. At least I should say, until a lot later in life.

Over time I got to know all the members that were members at the time and a lot that were past members. Some were life members, which meant they had done ten years in the club and by doing so had qualified themselves for life membership. Life membership came with the luxury of not having to be there all the time and only being involved to a lesser degree. It was not a full-time life you could say. But I knew most of the guys and gradually became more and more accepted. I knew how to keep quiet; I knew how to do my chores; I brought a few people around and I could exist in their world. I guess a major part of it was that I liked them, the life and the bikes. You must like what you are doing and who you are with otherwise it is not going to work. I think that is a well-accepted theory. To top that off I spent a lot of time there. I was there all the time; I liked these guys. Hard as it might be for some to relate to there were times when a lot of fun was had.

From the president at the top down the hierarchy to the prospect at the bottom everyone was different but obviously many of the guys had a lot in common. They were likeminded in a lot of ways. The president was a massive guy when I first met him. A real big dude dressed like a biker with long hair and beard, that like him, was massive. His hair was a great big mat of blond that draped off his head down and around his shoulders. He was a quiet guy, and you could tell he was not to be messed with. Sergeant-at-arms was a massive guy too. Short dark hair and a face that most people feared. He definitely was an evil looking guy or at least a mean looking guy anyway. That kind of face that was so weathered it kind of looked like leather. Then there were some of the other hard men in the club that I got to know. A set of blood brothers who were both very capable men, and another really old-school guy who had previously been in a different club before he joined these guys. He was covered in tattoos and even had an artificial limb. You would think by the looks of him that he had been a gang member since he was like ten years old, just every inch of his body was covered in ink, even his head. Just a hard man. The Māori member was a very tough guy too and he'd been a member for a long time. He was good. Hedge was another one who was a good guy. Then there was the other set of blood brothers, both long time members and old-school. Another couple of guys who were members for only a shorter period but were both well-known guys, Dug and Stick. They were both nice guys in my opinion. Not the mean looking type but rather your typical blue-collar guys with a pleasant attitude and a big love for the club. Plus, the guys I already mentioned like Miller, Uncle, and Dougal. There were all types and as I said a good number of members, life members and ex-members that were still close associates. It was a big enough group and for many years in Christchurch they kept a reputation for being a dangerous bunch who you didn't want to cross. The clubhouse was owned by the club and the extended family throughout Christchurch was widespread. This was a far-reaching network, the extent of which I would not properly know for several years to come.

One dark night in one of the inner suburbs of Christchurch there was a party going on which several of us attended. It was a party at the well-known Macey's Road address. I believe there was probably one hundred people there and most people were drinking and trying to have a good night. Several of our club's members were there but also several Devil's Henchmen members and of course a lot of supporters and regulars to the Macey's Road address. I noticed that on this occasion there were quite a few young people as well who you would probably describe as Home Boys. They had the baggy jeans and the young peoples' trend going on. It just so happened that, as we were gathered around waiting for some of the other guys to have their conversations, one of these Home Boys came up to me and started talking. I am not sure why, but it seemed as though he was totally oblivious to the people with whom I had just arrived. I think he thought I was just a straggler there on my own, or for whatever reason, he obviously decided that he was in a safe enough position to challenge me. Maybe he didn't see the patch members standing only a couple of meters away from me who I was with but, in any case, the first words that came out of his mouth and the way he said it sounded as though he had come over to start a fight. He said to me "I should really be doing something after what your people have done to mine." He was a Māori guy, and he obviously had an issue with the white people verses Māori people scenario for at least that particular moment in time. I cannot say what his general philosophy regarding historical events was the rest of the time because I didn't know him but on this occasion, he had a problem about something. And I was really the wrong person to be talking to about it because I was obviously just a boy at the time, all of fifteen years old. I really don't think I knew anything about anything with regards to what he was talking about. One thing I do know is that he was suggesting that I was somehow involved and that he would be within his rights to act upon this grievance. I did not say anything to him; I just looked at him.

The tension increased as soon as he said it, and it just so happened that one of the patch members standing close to me was the sergeant-at-arms. The sergeant-at-arms had a friend of his with him called Dave. I did not particularly like Dave. This guy always wore a business suit and he was a bit of a show-off. Dave would boast and try and make out like he was a member when really, he was nothing, just someone who knew someone, he certainly wasn't a member. So yes, he was a show-off and that would be a kind way of saying it, but in any case, Dave overheard this Māori guy say what he said to me, and Dave immediately put his nose in and basically encouraged us to go a step further. "He's picking a fight with you Huw," he said, "I'll watch your back mate, go for it."

So, I was now committed to this fight with this guy that I'd never met in my life before or even spoken a word to before. Again, not unusual and something that I would become familiar with over time. Without a second delay we were fighting, he being the bigger guy made an early attempt at a swing of some sort, but because we were standing so close it immediately turned into a wrestle. I had thrown a lot of animals around out on the farm and played a lot of rugby so, as I previously said, I was conditioned

reasonably well to a bit of physical confrontation. Strong enough and probably clear headed enough due to the fact that I was sober, I was able to
make a quick decision. Obviously, I could not loose this fight with the guys
standing right there watching me, so I had to do something fast to end the
fight and subsequently appear to take the victory. This would mean doing
something to hurt him in a way that he would stop the fight. I do not recall
exactly why I did it or where I got the idea from because it just came to me
in a split second. But it just happened almost subconsciously, I stuck both
my thumbs deep into his eye sockets. He flopped over and curled up in
a ball immediately with a large crowd now standing around us watching.
That was it, not a very courageous, glamourous win, but it was a win and
that was all that mattered at that point in time. I think the people watching
might have been a bit confused actually. They probably hadn't seen me
throw a single punch and it's likely that in the split second it took to gouge
his eyes, they may not have seen that either, so they would have been left
wondering what had just happened. Funnily enough just as I was standing
there looking down at my opponent, a guy who was standing only a meter
away recognised me and said, "Huw".

I looked at him and realised it was a guy who was a year below me in
school. He had gone to Middleton Grange, the same school as I did, and
I had not seen him in several years. I'm guessing the year would have been
1993 or early 1994 and a number of years later that same guy went on
to become mildly famous throughout New Zealand. He was an Islander
but obviously he had grown up in New Zealand. I think he is of Samoan
decent. It was a strange encounter though, here I was standing next to a guy
I had been at school with and considering the formation and look of these
guys who all seemed to be lingering around together, the likelihood is that
this guy was an associate of the guy who was now laying on the ground in
front of me holding his now very sore eyes. Nothing else was said and by

this stage any friends of this guy on the ground who may have been thinking about retaliating would have seen the patch members standing there backing me up and decided it wasn't worth their worry getting involved. So we slowly moved away leaving this guy on the ground. I am aware now that eye gouging involves a high risk of eye injury, but I did not know this at the time. My defence would obviously be that he was the aggressor and the first to initiate the physical altercation thus forcing me into a position requiring the use of force to prevent my own personal injury. Basically, it was self-defence. I would hope though that such a silly incident did not cause long term injury to this guy. As it happens, I've never heard of or seen him ever again. Truth be known I would not recognise him anyway, even if he was standing right in front of me, it was that long ago.

That was my first proper fight since I had begun spending time with the club. It was certainly the first time they were watching me. Obviously, I was relieved because it was one of those times when you had to win. Loosing was just not an option during those times especially when you are in a relatively public environment such as that. So, for the rest of the night, it would have been more of the usual drinks and smoking and standing around listening to the older guys. We turned up to quite a few different parties over the years at Macey's Road. There was always something reasonable going on there. They had a lot of parties over there and although none of the owners of the property were club guys they were known around the town, and it was a known party house. There would be strippers there, always large crowds, drinks for sale, bands playing and people partying into the small hours. One other night I was there I remember it got so late that two of our club's members and one Henchmen were all still drinking as daylight approached and they were all inside a caravan with this woman. I was in there too and it was pretty relaxed while we were just hanging onto a stubby (small glass bottle of beer) each and listening to the music that was still playing. A bit of chatter was going on in the caravan, the Henchmen was just joking around a bit with a bit of light-hearted humour, but one of the members of our club took it personally and suddenly erupted into a rage throwing his stubby behind him and hitting the Henchmen with it.

The Henchmen and our club member immediately locked into a fight at close quarters while another member of our club came in straight away to break them up because they were supposed to be friends. I was sitting there watching this all unfold at the age of about fifteen and it was definitely a bit of a surprise because I'd never seen them fight each other before. By this stage both our club member and the Henchmen were fuming and the second club member was trying to break them up. Bottles were flying and arms and legs were everywhere with more than one guy getting cut and bruised. There were a few big hits put in before it all quietened down and my club friend stormed out of the caravan door. My other friend from our club was riled up as well, because he'd been trying to break it up, but had still managed to get a cut above the eye from a bottle. The Henchmen was in there with us too wondering what had just happened after it had all started out of nothing. I was still sitting there with my stubby having not moved an inch from the time that it had started. But that was the way it went, and I'm sure it was talked about afterwards in a meeting or two. They would have sorted it out and life went on. The Henchmen member and our club were still friends; they were all still friends thereafter. Out of interest that Henchmen member was actually not such a bad guy. I remember him being around for years. Long hair and a long beard, I hardly ever saw him without his patch and his bike. Twenty odd years on from that party the Henchmen member having lived his life the same way from start to finish, slowed right down due to health issues which finally got the better of him. He was laid to rest a few years ago I believe and would be missed by quite a few people.

The nights and days rolled on and things progressed as they always do. More parties, rides, guys turning up at the clubhouse who I'd never met before and even the odd, stranger club turning up which I'd never have expected to be visiting our clubhouse. One morning I woke up to the sound of a front end loader smashing over the front gate. It was a police raid, and the gate was so heavily fortified they needed a loader that would have weighed over ten tonne to get over the steel bar in the ground and push the gate off its hinges before heavily armed police officers and members of the armed offenders squad poured through the gap made by the loader. They swarmed up the driveway and positioned themselves all around the house before entering through the saloon doors and making their way throughout the building holding everyone at gun point. I was still upstairs waking up and heard them yelling at us to surrender as they made their way through the house. There was no point resisting as there were too many and there was no reason to anyway. We all just filed downstairs and were placed in separate areas while they carried out a search of the property. The police are always very thorough when conducting a search such as this and, as I watched them go through every square inch of the property, many thoughts bounced around in my consciousness, but I do remember feeling relatively unperturbed about their presence. I believed the club was well prepared for times such as this. Police raids on gang houses were a common occurrence throughout New Zealand and it was just a matter of time before they would turn up again for their yearly or even six-monthly search. For that reason, it would be uncommon for large amounts of drugs or contraband to be kept at the club house. The members were highly schooled on how to avoid issues with the law and, while other gangs around the countryside were far less organised and sophisticated, our club were known for being well organised and always one step ahead of the law. Other gangs would have serious issues with numerous members going in and out of prison on a regular basis and for long periods of time, but this club seldom had members incarcerated. They did go to jail on numerous occasions, of course, and for varying lengths of time, but overall they didn't go as much as a lot of the other less organised gangs did such as the street gangs. The rule was if you're going to do something then you don't get caught because you're no good to anyone in there.

So, I knew this was just a routine visit and soon the police would pack up and depart leaving us to carry on with our unusual lives. And they did. Of course they wanted to know who I was and what my current address was but other than that there was nothing compelling myself or anyone else to give them any further information. On that occasion I believe they left with nothing, probably disgruntled and only satisfied with the fact that they'd destroyed the front gate and interrupted our lives.

I had been told of instances in the past where things had not run as smoothly, such as the times when police had pursued the entire club on their bikes back to the clubhouse whereupon a full-scale brawl had erupted between police and club members. Apparently, it was quite a while before my time and in those earlier days life was a little simpler. You could get away with things like that back then when between ten and twenty police came up against an even larger number of members and supporters. Punches raining from every direction, people being dropped on their heads and rammed into fences with all participants on both sides coming out battered and bruised. I heard of even more serious instances than that too where people were incarcerated as a result, but as I said things had changed since my arrival and so during that time you basically didn't want to push the boundaries too much when police were involved. Don't bring too much illegal contraband onto the premises and try not to draw too much attention to yourself, with the idea being that law enforcement will hopefully leave you alone.

As it turned out this theory would not be as easy to maintain as it sounds. I certainly learnt that lesson fast and in the not-too-distant future. But for now, life went on as usual. More drinking, riding and as some would say living the life. In hindsight almost comical events would crop up from time to time. I had a small group of friends that were all my age or a little older from outside the club circle and I brought a few of them around and introduced them to the club life. I actually fell for a beautiful young lady whom I first met through Uncle and Shell and then at a later stage I reconnected with her in town. Rachel and her friends would come to the club and hangout with us and do a little partying. The scene was quite exciting for them too, being a part of the adult's world and doing what you're not supposed to do. On one occasion she and her friend Brony came to the clubhouse to visit me. I heard the gate buzzer ringing, and I was trying to get the Hellhound around the back behind the locked gate so I could let the girls in the front gate, but the Hellhound wouldn't budge off the couch out the front where he was sitting. A little over-enthusiastically I tried to coax him around to the kennel while the girls stood waiting for me to open up. He wouldn't move so I picked up a pillow and threatened him with it. Suddenly he lunged at me and in a split second latched onto my hand before he let go and jumped back up onto the couch. Blood oozed out from my newly inflicted wound as I stood there and wondered what to do next. Then it came to me, bread. I rushed inside and grabbed a few slices of bread and lured him around to the kennel by dropping bits in front of him as he went. It worked, so I quickly shut the gate behind him and went out to greet the girls as if nothing had ever happened. And there began another sunny day at the clubhouse with my friends.

That Hellhound certainly was a vicious dog. I think he bit or attacked about eleven different people during his time at the clubhouse. On one occasion the sergeant-at-arms had bent down to about head height with the dog and let out a playful woof. With that the Hellhound bit him on the nose and nearly took it clean off. For years after you could see the stitch marks running down either side of my friend's nose. Hellhound was a really bad dog. I had learnt my lesson and after that I was always incredibly careful. There is more to the story of the Hellhound, and it is a little sad in the end but maybe I'll leave that story for another time.

Soon I was saving for my first bike. The guys told me I could get a nice Triumph Bonneville for around $3000 so that became my target and I put money away each week to make that happen. It would not be long before I was riding alongside them.

In the meantime, I kept on partying and learning the life. Day after day for months on end it was more of the same. I recall my younger friends coming around and partying with me a lot. They too had been accepted by this stage because of their connection through me but also because they were not there all the time like I was. They'd just come on the weekends, and they weren't really subjected to anything overly criminal. So as long as they minded their own business and didn't make a fool of themselves, they were allowed. For the first time we were introduced to acid (LSD), the hallucinogenic drug that became famous through its use in the sixties and seventies. We liked this kind of thing and yes in those early days it seemed okay. Just the feeling of escaping reality and laughing for hours and hours. In hindsight they did seem like innocent times and we were having fun, but unfortunately it was time that I probably should have been using for more constructive projects. I know this now, but hey with myself and a number of my friends being fatherless and basically without the right role models we did what we saw fit and that's the way it went. The drinking was very heavy too. Most nights on the weekends if I wasn't doing something else, I'd be drinking, and you'd just drink until you blacked out. I often woke up totally unaware of what had happened for the last couple of hours before

I'd finally crashed out. Sometimes you'd just wake up and think what on earth did I do last night, oh no, then the guilt comes on as small pieces of your memory came back to you. Of course, the thing to do was just to carry on and live another day. It was crazy times though. Everyone had their own taste in music and that varied from Led Zeppelin, The Doors, Rolling Stones through to heavy metal and sometimes the less intense sounds like Bob Dylan and Neil Young. Two entire walls behind the bar were stacked with cassette tapes of all kinds. Literally thousands of tapes and that shows you how long ago it was too. All tapes, no CDs or internet back then. In fact, there were not even cell phones back in those days, the only phone being a landline which was in an out of the way phone booth with a big sign hanging over it that said, "Say nothing on the phone".

The parties got more and more out of control the longer I lived there and one day we all got so drunk and comfortable with each other's company we somehow broke off into two teams, members on one side and prospects/supporters on the other side of the bar and it turned into a full-on bottle war. Uncle and a few others were just hurling these big bottles at us, and we started firing them back across the room. Big bottles I had thrown smashing against the bar within inches of Uncle and co and in return they were nearly hitting us. It would have looked serious to anyone watching but we were all laughing while we were doing it. It went on for minutes and by the end of it there was glass and ash trays strewn throughout the building. Of course, I was the one who had to clean it up the next day, but I'm pretty sure I wasn't concerned. I can remember the comradery and the brotherhood I felt with these people around me. There were moments where we really had some good times together.

The action did not always take place inside the club building either. The property around the club was fairly spacious and there was a balcony out the front underneath the trees. The long driveway where the bikes were always parked stretched to the back of the property where the bike sheds and Hellhound's kennel was. During the meetings I would always hang out in the shed with the prospects while we waited for news from inside.

There was a watch tower at the front which overlooked the street and often we'd stand up there for hours on end mostly enjoying ourselves and talking into the night. Obviously, it was there for a reason and at times we'd be up there keeping a look out. While I was living there they lined all the inside of the driveway fence with the steel walls either from a shipping container or some other very heavy steel reinforcement. The fence around the remainder of the property was sand bagged up to head hight to stop bullets coming through the fence. I was standing on top of the sandbags one day holding onto the iron fence when the sandbags fell away underneath me, and I went plummeting towards the ground ripping my hand open on the iron fence and peeling a chunk of flesh off from the palm of my hand. Not one of my smartest moments, but one that stuck in my memory for some reason. Probably one of those days when I'd had too much to drink.

So that's how it carried on for quite a long time and it all seemed relatively harmless. Not the big scary world of biker gangs that most people would have imagined. But unfortunately, it wouldn't always be like that. Things were going to change soon and the trouble I would eventually get myself into was already starting to brew.

CHAPTER 6

PROSPECT

t was 1994 and I was now sixteen years old. I had been saving my money for quite a while and very soon I would have enough to get into my own bike. A couple of the guys were starting to talk to me about earning money and made it clear to me that money was a fairly important factor when it came to staying afloat in this world. The problem was I did not spend a lot of time with the guys who worked full time jobs, so all I really knew about making money was what I had seen from the members who weren't working. Obviously, the way they made money was through what Uncle referred to as wheeling and dealing. A number of the members were full time workers and were involved in plumbing, welding, bike repairs and various other legitimate activities, but obviously if you're in full time employment you don't have a lot of time to be hanging around the club-house and spending time with a young hang-around like myself. So, I spent time with Uncle, the sergeant-at-arms, Dougal and a few of the other guys who had the time to spare. These guys were on the dole and doing whatever else they could to make a buck. Some of them had income coming in through their wives or girlfriends as well. Typically the income that came in paid your bike payments, rent and living supplies. Basically, you would be working away on other projects at the same time, trying to either pull in a big haul all at once or simply increase what you already had coming in. I sometimes wish that during those early days I could have had some family members around me or a little more encouragement to get on the right track, but it wasn't to be. My dad was dead, mum's father was dead, and my older brother was at university studying classical music. I had three uncles but for whatever reason they were always pretty busy looking after their own families. One lived in the South, the other in the North Island, and the only one that was in Christchurch was an accountant who I rarely had anything to do with. I don't think he would have been able to help much anyway at that stage because his world just seemed so totally different to the world I was living in. Basically, my family were more of the educated professional types and that was quite different to the way I was living. A rich uncle who owned a big machinery contracting business might not have gone astray in those days, but it wasn't to be, and the only work experience I had under my belt was the farm work which wasn't really a big earner when you entered at ground level. Perhaps I could have stuck it out farming or put more effort in at the times when I was out working on the farms, but right at that point in time, I was pretty much hooked into the club scene anyway and the reality is I was getting by on what I had. I should have listened more and taken the moneymaking advise more seriously, but because I was young and just interested in the pleasures of life, I neglected the more important aspects. I saw the older guys with bikes, drugs, and girls and that's really all I wanted too. As time went by the need for money certainly increased, but still the urgency just wasn't quite there yet. It would come but not for a while.

Another reason for my lack of progress with moneymaking was also because I was reckless and careless. A great example of this would be the time I got into trouble right next to the clubhouse. Rick and I were spending time together this particular day and I had become so intoxicated I pretty much lost control of my thinking and for whatever crazy reason, I hurled a seven-inch lump of concrete through a car window and hit an innocent person in the head. I was in deep trouble straight away. I seriously did not mean to hit anyone I don't think and from the distance I threw it I guess I was assuming that it might hit the car and just bounce off but it went through the side window and hit them. Very bad luck for them and me. I shot back into the clubhouse and was immediately told to sit down while the guys established what had happened. Shortly after the president came up to me and smacked me right in the jaw knocking me back into a sitting position. I knew I was an idiot and within just a few minutes I think I sobered up amazingly fast. The guys were lingering around wondering what to do and I just sat there regretting what I'd just done.

It was near to the clubhouse and the cops turned up in a couple of different cars. The poor, innocent person was being attended to on the side of the road, but fortunately they weren't badly injured. This was seriously not a good look and I had just broken the main rule of not drawing attention to ourselves. The best thing I could do was go outside and confront the situation and take responsibility before it got any worse, so that's what I did. Luckily for me the police weren't too hard on me and, for whatever reason, possibly because I was only sixteen they felt a bit of compassion for me and didn't lay the charges on thick. I think one of the older club guys may also have spoken on my behalf and just told them I was a silly young punk and that perhaps they could go easy on me because I didn't know what I was doing. I'm not sure what was said exactly but, in any case, the cops were pretty reasonable.

I was still arrested though and taken away on charges of disorderly behaviour or something along those lines. Whatever the charges were though they weren't serious and after a short stay in the holding cells I was released on bail with the instruction that I should appear in court on a certain day and time. Back at the club I was told off again. At the meeting a few days later I was told that if I did something stupid like that again I'd be gone from the club. That was my first warning. Don't bring attention to the club. At the court appearance a short time later things went my way again and because it was my first time in trouble with the law, I was given diversion which means no criminal history would be recorded against my name. I would hate to think what charges an incident like that would bring against you in this day and age. Gee it was lucky.

The next significant event that took place was the purchase of my first bike. The club guys used the money I had saved to purchase me my first Triumph Bonneville. A dark blue, 1971, 650 Triumph Bonneville. Man did I love that bike. Great look, great sound and it just went so well. I learned to ride that Bonne before I even learnt to drive a car and in fact, I had that motor bike on the road for at least a couple of years before I got my first car. I rode it every day and I rode it everywhere I needed to go. I had no licence, but that didn't stop me. If I had to go somewhere I simply went. I did make plans to get it at some stage, but I can't remember when that might have been. Once I was good enough at riding, I was allowed to join in on the club rides too. Always at the back and being fairly careful, of course, as I went. Great feeling being out there doing it with the other guys. Because the Bonne was only a 650, I definitely struggled to keep up especially out on the open roads. The bigger Triumph's, Ducati's and Harley's were a lot faster, but nevertheless it was still awesome fun, and I wouldn't normally be too far behind at the end of a ride; they were all still within sight.

Things were about to suddenly change within our world and the only people who knew about it were the members. I would imagine that, like myself, most family and supporters were totally oblivious to what was about to happen. One day I turned up at the clubhouse and all the members were there and they were wearing a different set of colours. They were now wearing a completely different patch. Everyone was there except for a couple of the life members.

It was definitely a big surprise and, according to what I was told, the move was for several different reasons. It was by no means a takeover because everyone considered our club to still be very strong and even dominant. The fact is though, other clubs were growing fast and the "numbers game" was to blame for it. That is the desire to expand quickly and have a lot of members. The Road Knights for example had chapters in Invercargill, Dunedin, Timaru and Christchurch. The Devils Henchmen had chapters in Christchurch and Timaru. Other clubs also had numerous clubhouses in the North and South. These different clubs also had a lot of members. One in Christchurch would have had twice the number of members as our club. Having said that, the reason I stated that our club was still dominant among clubs is because the members of ours were considered very staunch. The reputation was that they were dangerous, and the reality is they were in fact dangerous. So even though the new club may have had twice as many members, the fact is that our club was still considered by many as the more dangerous of the two. So, the real reason our club went with the new club from my understanding is for the purposes of expansion. They would now be a part of a group that owned multiple clubhouses in different parts of New Zealand. Also, they would be part of a much bigger group as far as numbers went. I guess it was about keeping up with the times. The club members of old will tell you the reason they didn't expand a lot prior to this merger was because they liked to keep it "small and tight". And they did for decades do just that and they did it very well. They had a highly effective group of guys and stood their ground for a long time. Not only that but they also had contacts and friends all over the country as well as in Christchurch. The club was well respected by many throughout the country. But as the race for numbers, property and money heated up it had to follow suit. Or at least that is what everyone believed anyway.

The new club by this stage was getting a bit busier; there was an influx of new guys on the scene who all arrived around the same time. I have already mentioned my big friend Rick and then there were three other guys who arrived. All four started prospecting around the same time. I was still just a hang-around at the age of sixteen but these guys who arrived were all in their twenties and thirties and had known the members for long enough to become a prospective member. Being a prospect meant that you basically do what you were told for any number of months until the members considered you good enough to become a full patch member. There was Rick, Shorty (I have already mentioned Shorty), and two men I will call Harmen and Toppa. These guys would hopefully get through the prospecting stage and bolster the numbers even more making the expansion not only a sideways move but also internal. Four prospects at the same time was a good start, and in actual fact the number of members had increased anyway prior to the merger with the full patches being given to Miller and one of the two pleasant guys, Dug.

Then one day I arrived back at the clubhouse again for another surprise. This time it was a new half jacket for me with a side patch sown onto the front of it. I was being promoted into the role of a prospect and I was still only sixteen years old. This was a big deal for me and later I was told by Uncle that very rarely would anybody be allowed to prospect at such a young age. In fact, the only other person in the history of the club that had prospected at such a young age was the president. He had started prospecting at sixteen also and more than a decade later he had gone on to be the president. I wasn't sure if they were making a very wise decision trusting me with such a responsibility but heck I wasn't going to disagree. So, I willingly took on the role and things carried on from there. Not a lot changed as far as the work I did around the clubhouse because I was already doing the work of a prospect before they promoted me, but it did mean that whenever I went out, I was now officially representing the club even though it was just in the role of a prospect. So, you had to keep things together because people would know who you were and if they didn't already know it was easy enough to find out. Simple stuff I guess but it does get a bit difficult when drugs or alcohol are involved. In a way the fact that I didn't have lots of money at the time probably kept me safe to a certain degree because I spent more time at the clubhouse and wouldn't be out in the public eye or putting myself in a position where things could have got out of hand.

Spending time at the club was also helpful with regards to earning your way towards a full patch. The prospects were required to be at the club for a certain number of hours every week and most of the guys would do their time and then head back to their own place or their girlfriend's. Since I lived at the clubhouse it made it a lot easier for me because, unless I was out on a mission or doing some chore, then you would generally find me at the clubhouse. This meant I was putting in twice as much time as the other prospects. Having said this, I really didn't expect to get my colours any faster no matter how much time I put in because it was a big enough surprise for me to just be given my prospect patch, let alone a full patch. I was expecting that I would be prospecting for at least two years. I still felt like a young kid so I didn't see how I would be given a set of colours any time in the foreseeable future. That was just my internal feelings. But for whatever reason that didn't seem to matter to me, I think I was just happy to be there and be involved.

They did make some positive comments though about my work. One time there would have been between forty or fifty guys at the club all drinking and smoking before a ride and when they left the ash trays were full and there was bottles everywhere and ash on the floor and the general mess left after a big crowd has been hanging around. I cleaned it all up in about forty minutes and I remember these visitors who I'd never met before commenting on the clean up effort and complimenting my attitude. I heard things like that from time to time. Another time the member with the artificial limb had congratulated me in front of a few people after I had a fight with Shorty for being what he considered a "staunch prick". Even though Shorty, who was twelve years my senior and a lot bigger at the time, had got the better of me the member said I deserved respect standing up for myself straight away without stopping to think about it. That was a good compliment that I appreciated. So, I wasn't too bad at my job, and I got a little bit of appreciation for my efforts.

A couple of times when the members were all drinking and the night was getting on, they had what they called a "prospect challenge". Basically, we had to race to beat each other, and this made for good entertainment for everyone who was partying. On one of these occasions, we had ridden down to a Timaru clubhouse for a big party. The race involved several of us, probably as many as half a dozen prospects. To start the race, they were going to blow the horn and then we were all supposed to eat a raw onion, scull a half jug of beer and then run across the good-sized yard, climb the watch tower and touch the top rail before climbing back down and running back across the yard and across the finish line. They blew the horn, and everyone started eating their onion. I can tell you that that was a lot harder than I thought it would be and before I got even a quarter of the way through it, I started throwing up. I looked and the other guys were already drinking the jugs and then they were running as well. All the while I'm still standing there eating a little bit and then throwing up and then eating a little bit more and trying to wash it down with a drink and then I'd throw up again. It was nearly impossible, and I was still standing there trying to eat the onion when all the other guys were climbing back down from the watch tower and running back across the finish line. I thought I'd lost the race spectacularly, but then the members declared me the winner because all the others were disqualified for not eating the onion which explains why they took off so fast. So, I won, because I followed the instructions.

CHAPTER 7
SIGNIFICANT EVENTS

My day-to-day routine during this time revolved around partying, riding, prospecting and getting my tasks done around the clubhouse. I was not thinking about any higher power, I was not thinking about God. Only occasionally out of the blue might I stop for a moment to mull over thoughts of an eternal life. Living a moral life was not something I aspired to at this point in time. A few years later a significant event would take place that would change the way I thought for ever. I will explain this event further on down the track and, although it may seem trivial to some readers, it was like an instant revelation at the time. An unlocking of something that had been missing for many years. That was my turning point and, even though the turn around actually took some time to come about, it did eventually happen.

In the meantime, there was a lot of water still to go under the bridge. So, my days were much of the same as I have already explained previously. I guess people would be expecting the hectic events and dramas to be occurring whilst the club was in full swing and I was living at the clubhouse as a prospect, but this was not necessarily the case. The times were in a way boring and non-consequential. That is once you get over gang member processions on bikes, parties, police, and the odd brawl and so forth.

Prior to my arrival at the club there had been numerous significant events that took place. I had been told about them and they ranged from warfare with the Christchurch Black Power street gang and included our club shooting and stabbing members of the Black Power on several different occasions through to mid-level corruption cases that involved employees of the Christchurch district court. There were reports of missing persons, high profile drugs busts and even accusations of white supremacy by the media. The latter was strange considering our club had members, wives, and associates who were of Māori decent. A lot had gone on in the twenty odd years before I arrived on the scene and to list all the events would probably give the impression of an overly dramatic lifestyle, but I guess when you are living that life it doesn't always seem to be like that. Going back a decade into the 1980's I do know that the club was a lot bigger. They had twice as many members in the 80's and so yes there definitely would have been more going on back then. In the 90's when I was involved, there weren't as many members and the members that were there had obviously matured and so yes things were probably a little quieter. In any case, as I said looking back it didn't seem that hectic, at least when I was there anyway. There were however a few events that took place that stand out in my memory. One event that made headlines was the murder of Angela Blackmore.

Angela Blackmore, a young woman from the suburb of Wainoni was murdered on August the 17th 1995. According to news reports she was pregnant at the time and had a two-year-old son asleep in the next room. Angela was reportedly stabbed 39 times and beaten with a bat. Police raided our clubhouse not long after this incident occurred. According to police they had received information leading them to believe that we were somehow involved. I was at the clubhouse when they came, and it was a raid and search typical of any other search I had been through. The exception being that this time they were asking questions of everyone regarding where each of us had been on the night in question. I really cannot remember how the conversations went with police but since I knew nothing I was not at all concerned about their questioning. In fact at the time the police raided, I didn't even know that this murder had occurred, let alone why they were at the club this particular day. I do know though that the members were very unhappy about this raid and subsequent media reporting because it showed photographs of the clubhouse and identified our club. Everyone that I knew who was involved with the club at the time and who I have spoken to in recent years denied any knowledge of, or any involvement in, this crime. Several conversations I have had with the old President were always along the same lines of anger towards police for their willingness and persistence in pursuing investigations along club lines. It was plastered all over the media and police continued their interest into our club's possible involvement for years to come. Even in the late 2000's police were still looking into this when they left a calling card at my residence requesting that I call them. At this time I was still involved in the scene and activities so I really didn't want to hear from Police. After taking advice from one of the older members it was decided that I could simply front up and answer their questions and then leave. The member, who maintained a presence as an authority figure among us, suggested that if I didn't know anything and I wasn't going to give them any information relating to anything else then there was no reason why I couldn't go in and "get them off my back". So that's exactly what I did, I went in, I saw them, and I told them I knew nothing about it. I genuinely did not know anything whatsoever about this case other than what was already in the news.

The detectives involved with my interview suggested that some mystery person had told them that I had told this person that I was sitting in the car outside the property while this murder took place. It was a load of rubbish and I do not know why the police said this to me. In hindsight

I have surmised that police may have listened to a voice recording of me talking about some other incident where I said I was sitting in the car and because in the recording I made no mention of what incident it was, police had just taken a wild guess and thought well perhaps he was talking about that murder. If I am correct in that they did listen to a voice recording, the reason they would not have heard which incident I was talking about is because I would have been using sign language or mouthing the missing words so that no one other than my friends would know what I was talking about. That was very common among us because you would basically assume they were always listening. Anyway, I told the police that their suggestion was ridiculous because what insane person would take a sixteen- or seventeen-year-old along with them to commit a murder. Secondly I said why would anyone tell a seventeen-year-old anything about it as well. I said you're "totally barking up the wrong tree" and that I was a respectable person nowadays. I was telling the truth except for the part about being a respectable person because that was still a work in progress. I was trying to be a respectable person, but I wasn't quite there yet.

That murder became a cold case murder and went unsolved for more than twenty years. A woman and a man were arrested in 2019 and charged with murder after a reward for $100,000 was offered to the public for information leading to a conviction. Jeremy Powell, 45 and Rebecca Wright-Meldrum, 48, were arrested in October of 2019. This would have made the two killers approximately 21 and 24 at the time of the murder. Then in 2020 a second man was charged. As far as I am aware, I do not know either of the first two arrested, but I do know the third person. His name is David Hawken. I can confirm that none of these people were members of our club and from what I have been told by one club figure the first two were definitely not connected to the club. David Hawkin, however, was an associate of the sergeant-at-arms, and this is how I knew him. David

Hawken was the guy I mentioned earlier who had been at the party with us at Macey's Road. This was the same Dave who had encouraged the fight between me and the other young guy which resulted in me eye gouging him. So, it turns out after all these years, that I did know one of the killers. Not very well though, as I previously said I didn't really like Dave and I don't think I was alone in that regard. Dave was just one of a large number of people who knew someone. It just so happened that he knew the sergeant-at-arms, but this was really a fairly insignificant fact, because a quarter of Christchurch know someone either directly or indirectly. This wasn't really a big thing and I know Dave was not a big club supporter or anything like that. I knew who the big club supporters were, I was one of them and there were lots of others too, but Dave wasn't one of them. It just so happened that he was hanging around with the sergeant-at-arms about the same time that the murder happened. There was one other connection and that was the ex-husband of Angela Blackmore. According to reports the sergeant-at-arms knew William Blackmore and at some stage had been a flatmate in the same house as him. But I think this only occurred as a result of the two being connected through David Hawken. And I'm not sure when this might have been because the entire time that the clubhouse was operating, I remember the sergeant-at-arms was always living upstairs in his own room. I always thought he lived there permanently. But in any case, he was never charged, and neither was any other member of The Club.

It appears as though William and Angela still owned a house together and at the time of the murder the two were trying to negotiate a deal whereby William would buy Angela out. David Hawken was supposably at the centre of these negotiations and was also living in the house at the time, while Angela and William lived elsewhere. Reports suggest that David had loaned the two up to $10,000 to help with mortgage payments but since then had fallen on hard times and obviously needed his money back.

Jeremy Powell admitted to the murder, but Rebecca Wright-Meldrom and David Hawkin are still pleading not guilty at the time I am writing this and have yet to appear for trial. In the summary of facts Jeremy Powell was said to have travelled to the house on the night of the murder and carried out the attack. He has claimed he was paid $10,000 for the job, but it is unclear whether he ever received the payment. So, with no summary of facts available relating to Hawken and Wright-Meldroms involvement due to the fact that they have yet to face trial I would only be guessing as to what part they actually played. Possibly Wright-Meldrom was there on the night that it happened and I'm assuming the police have tied David Hawken to the payment offered. Apparently David has been cleared of any physical involvement as he had a sound alibi on the night of the incident.

This was a big case at the time. A young pregnant mother who left behind a partner and probably other family members as well. I certainly don't know exactly what went on and it's difficult without any connection to them to understand a great deal about their lives and the subsequent damage this has caused the grieving family. But it's obvious that major damage was caused, and any rational person would likely have been able to resolve the issues without the loss of life. Like any story though there will be goings on in the background which we may never know about. Over the years when I read some of the articles and looked at the pictures in the media reports I struggled to even imagine any connection this woman might have had to our club. I just couldn't see how she would have been important enough to anyone I know to murder her. We know now that, although her new partner appears to have lived a normal life, Angela herself had lived a very troubled life from a young age and had become involved with drugs and prostitution before meeting her new partner. But even so they didn't appear to be the type of people to have anything to do with us. I had never, ever seen Angela or her partner at the clubhouse or any other social gathering. She was, however, unfortunate enough to know Dave and that would lead to her end.

In hindsight this significant event probably had a substantial impact on our club as we knew it. When something like that goes down and police wrongly or rightly believe you were involved, I can tell you they will not leave you alone from that moment on and the police were already intensely interested in our club well before this happened. So, from that point on you could say that police scrutiny intensified by tenfold for at least a time and, without knowing all the goings on of all the individual members and associates, I can at least say that this would have made everybody extremely uncomfortable. I believe this single event could have contributed to the conclusion of the original club. It was at least a contributing factor.

When I first started prospecting there were as many as five prospects including myself who were prospecting at the same chapter in Riccarton. In a short space of time that number dropped right down until I was the only prospect left, which you could also say was another significant event. Obviously, it was an event that was nowhere within the scope of the afore mentioned event but in any case, it was something that made a big difference as far as our club was concerned.

I can't remember in which exact order everybody dropped off, but I still recall how it happened. Toppa took off one day never to return. He left his Moto Guzzi bike parked in the driveway and, as far as I am aware, nobody ever heard from him again. I guess the lead up to this was that he was never really a very pleasant person. I do know he made a few mistakes prior to his departure and let's just say that it was probably a wise move for him to take off as he did, otherwise he might have found himself in a bit of hot water once the news had gotten out about what he'd been up to. To cut a long story short, I heard he had found some drugs in the driveway one night and instead of handing them in to the members he had just pocketed them, which as you can understand would have been seen as dishonest. And that was not even really serious, unlike the fact that he made an advance one night onto the wrong woman. I was there when he did it and that I can definitely say, was serious. It was definitely bad enough for him to become immediately paranoid and make his departure. Shorty also went after his bike accident, no mystery regarding that one. Harmen packed it in, and I don't know why exactly other than it was something to do with needing to be there for his family, which was understandable. And finally, my good friend Rick went too. Again, I think it was to do with family and being unable to fully commit to club life. So that just left me by myself as the lone prospect for the Riccarton chapter. Don't get me wrong, prospects often came and went, and it was no big deal so again this wasn't major, but it is definitely worth a mention as it was an immediate reduction in the number of prospective members which would subsequently affect the future of our club.

The next event that took place was the night our club pulled out from their union with the other club. I can clearly remember the night it took place. It was a meeting night and I was outside as usual for meeting nights, and I could hear Dougal inside the meeting room yelling. I can only surmise what they were talking about on account of the fact that I was not filled in on the finer details, but I do know that the new patches came off everybody's jackets that very night. I was called into the meeting at the end and given the option of staying in Riccarton with our club or transferring over to the chapter of the other club on the opposite side of town. I didn't even take a second to think about it and I responded immediately stating that I would remain loyal to the original club and stay with them. There was no way I was transferring over to the others. I'd done my time with these guys and as far as I was concerned that's who I was too. I was one of them.

From what I was told our club were extremely dissatisfied with the others and most of those complaints appeared to stem from broken promises. Most likely those promises related to financial issues, but it is possible there were other aspects involved that I was not made aware of. In any case our club was taking off all their regalia as of that moment and was totally withdrawing from any union that had previously been in place. Our club would retain the clubhouse, all of the club's members including the lone prospect, and all properties and belongings that had previously belonged to our original club. In essence this was an aggressive rejection of the other club and its hierarchy. In any other normal circumstance, the patch wearing club would take on all ownership of all belongings of any of its chapters, both new and old, but obviously this wasn't going to be the case this time around. I do not know how they were notified of this separation, but I would imagine they knew straight away, and they would have been told how this was going to happen. They would have simply had to accept the terms because there wasn't any way they were going to go to war against our club. Whether we were wrong or right as far as political decision making went it didn't matter, because the Riccarton club had already made up their mind as to what they were doing, and nobody could stop them. The others were not in a position to dictate to our club and so they could only let us go on our terms and that was that.

There was one thing that could not happen though and that was a return to our club's original patch. Politically that was something that no club would ever do. Basically, once you take off your own original patch and put on another club's patch, there is no way you can ever go back to wearing your old patch. I do know there was talk about it, and definitely many members wanted to do that, but as I said it was something that was totally out of bounds, hence the reason it never made it past the point of conversation. There were suggestions of merging with another international club, in fact there were mutterings of a number of possible scenarios, but for the time being nothing was being set in concrete. For now, the club would still function as it had previously done except that now it was a club with no name and no patch.

Prior to the separation from the other club there had also been a couple of members who had stepped down from their roles. I think they weren't happy with the union and had decided that they no longer wanted to be involved. These guys were very important guys, so to say they were a loss would be a major understatement. One of them, in particular, was a corner stone to our original club and had been a member for well over ten years. He was a very staunch man too. There were a couple of life members who returned after the split to try and help out, so the numbers were not affected very much. Still the loss of two solid guys was not something anyone would have wanted, so again that was an unforeseen event that certainly didn't help.

For the next six to nine months the club continued having meetings, going on rides, and generally speaking they were getting on with things as per normal. In fact, there were a few massive parties that went on after the split and, to all intents and purposes, you would have thought something was definitely going to happen, but for whatever reason it just seemed to remain the same for some time. There was no decision on the future of the club.

I can't recall exactly why I decided to leave, but there would have been a multitude of thoughts going through my mind at the time. My mother and a couple of old family friends had been talking to me and discussing how I needed to plan for my future. That would have had some impact, but really I think that I may have lost interest due to the lack of activity going on at the club. I went into the meeting on the night that I left, after running my plan past Uncle, and simply told them I wanted to leave. I think I was attempting to motivate the guys into doing something. I told them that I didn't see any way forward for me there and that I was leaving on account of this. One of the guys snapped back at me, as he wasn't happy about it, but the reality was, they weren't going to do anything to me because to them I was still just a kid. I think a couple of them might have been a bit sad about it because they liked me being around. I'm sure a lot of the guys could sense that our club was winding down and so my departure was just another sign of the time. In my mind I never thought they would close the club down. It didn't occur to me that what I was doing was contributing to the end. I thought they would just keep going and that possibly, hopefully, they might stick the colours back on. Obviously, I liked the original colours but that was not the point as I just wanted to see something other than a line of leather jackets. I know that it wasn't my fault and that it was probably for the better, but I still regret the way I left that night. If I hadn't left things might have been different.

My mother had moved by this stage to a near-new unit on Brougham Street and there was enough room for me there, so I shifted back in with her. I had started attending a farm training program and began traveling out to Rangiora everyday on my Triumph Bonneville to where the program was running. Not long after this shift to my mother's I received a phone call from the sergeant-at-arms suggesting that I should head down to the clubhouse as he had something he needed to talk to me about. At first I was excited and immediately I thought I was about to receive some good news, but he quickly told me that it wasn't what I thought and that I should just come down and have a talk. So, I headed down to the club and went inside to see what was going on. Upon entering the bar, I could tell straight away that this was not a time of jubilation. Hedge was there, the sergeant-at-arms and a few of the other guys coming and going. There was a sombre mood about the place, and I was quietly informed that the property had been sold and that this was our last opportunity to have a quiet drink before the building came down. They were going to start demolishing the old clubhouse the very next day and the land underneath would be used for a new development. It was very hard to believe at the time and I don't think it really registered with me. I started to have a few drinks out of a keg and pondered the situation while the others sat quietly. Nobody was really talking.

It is very strange how sometimes when a significant event is sprung on you like this the immediate reaction is one of zero feeling and emotion. I did not really feel anything at all. Sometimes it seems like it might take years before the reality of a situation properly sinks in and, in this case, this is exactly what happened. To many readers I guess you might think oh well, that's a good thing, the gang is gone and now you can get on with your life, but unfortunately it was never going to be that simple. For a start we the club people, members, prospects, and supporters, were all still the same people. Yes, the clubhouse was gone, but we were still there and so the daily challenges we faced were still present. The tribal mentality was still there, and all our antisocial, self-destructive characteristics had not gone away. For me, I had lost the structure that had kept me relatively safe for several years and, in hindsight, I can see that it was like loosing another family and family home. Years later I can recall the loss still affected me and I looked back on those times wishing the clubhouse was still there. I even had bizarre dreams from time to time about the clubhouse still being there and I remember in my dreams I was always elated when I would find myself back there. I know there was some connection going on here, but I've never really worked out what the dreams were about. One time I was back there and the sergeant-at-arms was there and a few of the other guys but for some reason there was a massive hole in the roof. Like, half the roof was gone. Another time I dreamed that the clubhouse was still there and that it just hadn't been used for years and that some of the old guys would just come and go occasionally and that they simply hadn't decided what to do with it. Again, I remember the feeling of excitement that the house was still there. So strange, who knows what it was all about, but I guess it demonstrates the love I had for that place and the tribal phenomenon that occurred while I was there. Of course, it is always easier to look back on something and recall fond memories, which is likely a part of what has been happening here, but I certainly don't want to undercut the real-life experience that did occur. There was some good in that old club, I know this for a fact.

So, the clubhouse was gone, but not the members. I was still around and so were a lot of old supporters and the children of the members. It was still a big circle of people and within months of the clubhouse being sold people were already talking about restarting the club. We were all still the same people and everyone loved the club lifestyle, so it made perfect sense that nothing would really change in the mindset of those involved. Of course, small changes occurred as we moved into different areas and started new jobs but for a lot of us, especially the younger ones, things were only just getting started.

CHAPTER 8
THE UNDERWORLD REGIME

Cell phones were not common in those days, but everyone seemed to keep in contact easily. I knew where everyone was, and it was either a landline call or a short journey to catch up with whoever you wanted to see. The parties were still going on as well and, in some ways, you could say that the group was still very much together. The older original patch members were seen as the authority figures to us younger guys and everybody else who was hanging around became a part of the family in one way or another.

I was about eighteen when I decided I needed to take some time out of the city and get into some work. It had been quite a while since I had been working or involved in any training, so I was pretty keen to put my head down for a while and try and forge a way ahead. I got a job on a dairy farm that was owned by a female friend's father. That job lasted about a year and it was hard going, massive hours and not much pay. We would have easily been doing seventy hours per week and we only had every second weekend off. Due to complications on the farm with a malfunctioning rotary shed and a much larger than normal herd of first year milkers the days really dragged. The impression I got from my first year was not a good one. During that year I also headed back into town regularly and kept in contact with all of the circle. There were a few parties at Miller's house where a number of the older members were starting to hang out a bit. Miller had fortified his house a lot like a clubhouse with a heavy steel fence, gate and bar. Miller was a bit of a genius when it came to mechanics and machinery and also had his entire garage decked out with lathes and other engineering machinery. A while before I started working on the farm, my Bonneville had blown a hole in the piston and so Miller helped me put that back together at his place, which was another reason I was over there a bit during that period of time. In that same year I also met up with a couple of different woman. The first one hung around for a while but for some reason which I can't quite remember now I finished with her and met up with a new girlfriend who I would be with for a little while. The new girl Kate was a crazy, beautiful blond. She was also a pot head and an alcoholic, but I really didn't care in the slightest. That's where I was at the time, that's where my head was. She was twenty-three, beautiful and that's all I knew.

Looking back, I would have to say that this is one of the times in my life where I thought the least about the spiritual realm. I might have gone for months at a time without even thinking about God. Trying to think back to what I was thinking then is obviously not too easy but from my rough memory I think I would have been thinking about all the things that pleasured the flesh. Alcohol, woman, drugs and having a good time. It is hard to remember but I'm pretty sure I wasn't thinking about God at all. I was away in my own world you could say and possibly this was the early warning signs for the places I was about to go.

Prior to that first year on the farm, the old member Hedge had decided to leave Christchurch for Levin. He was offered an immediate set of colours in Levin with the Tyrants Motorcycle club. Because he'd been a member in Christchurch for a good number of years and our club had always been very close to the Tyrants, Hedge wouldn't have to prospect or anything like that. As soon as he got there, he was to be given his full patch. I went with Hedge up to Levin when he went. I was supposed to go for a couple of weeks. There was talk about me moving up there to prospect for them as well, but obviously that would be a big move for me so I couldn't guarantee that I would be up for it. I went with Hedge anyway and was there when he got his patch on arrival at the Levin clubhouse. Of the few times I went up to Levin I remember having some pretty crazy times. One time I was up there they had plates full of magic mushrooms and each time you had a handful you'd be completely gone for hours. At one stage I went into a bit of a panic not knowing how I would get home and trying to ring the Interislander Ferry when I was completely tripping off my head. Crazy times. But in any case, that is how I got to know a few of the Tyrants and obviously the Tyrants needed no introductions when it came to the older Christchurch guys. This is why the Tyrants were down visiting us and the Henchmen during that first year that I worked on the dairy farm.

So, it was around that time when the Tyrants were down and we were partying at a night club in town when I met the first girl I mentioned and then not long after that, that I met Kate. Kate and I got on alright and I would stay in town at her place from time to time and likewise she came out to Dunsandel where I was working to stay on the farm with me. Little did I know that she was soon to be embroiled in my first serious criminal case.

There were two separate attacks on a house in town over a period of a couple of weeks. I believe only the windows were smashed but the police blew it up in the media and called it a racist attack. The police blamed me for it and went around to Kate's house to question her about it. As they were walking up Kate's drive, they looked through the window and caught her with a pile of drugs she was planning to sell sitting on her kitchen table. According to Kate they immediately threatened to take her child off her if she didn't tell them what they wanted to hear, so she became a witness against me in the police case. The only evidence they had against me was what Kate had told them but that was an enough for an arrest.

Soon after the police arrested me and charged me with crimes relating to this incident. In court I plead not guilty and gave no statement to police. I had a lawyer straight away who got me bail and so for me the plan was basically to sit and wait and see what came of it. The fact is I was not a racist at all, I had Māori friends, I'd always had a few Māori friends, and as I previously stated there were Māori members and associates of the club. Even in those days to be a racist was not a cool thing and especially around the club where I'd spent most of my teenage years racism was not part of the culture. It just wasn't. Police labelled it as a racist crime because the victims at the premises where the attack occurred were not of New Zealand descent and were of a non-white ethnicity. The word on the street though was that this was not a racism thing. The word was that members of the house where the crime occurred became aggressive to certain people on the street one day and raised weapons in an attempt to intimidate them. The subsequent attacks were basically just a retaliatory warning to them not to do it again.

Around the time that I was arrested for this event, I had moved back into Christchurch. I'd left the farming job and found myself spending quite a bit of time back in town.

It wasn't long before I was in court again on trial for the incident police claimed I was involved with. I maintained my innocence, police put forward circumstantial evidence none of which tied me to the crime and Kate went hostile witness which put an end to the prosecution. The Judge had no choice but to find me not guilty and release me with no further court proceedings pending. That was that, I was a free man again.

That was my first proper run in with the law apart from the few misdemeanour crimes I'd already been up against, but it certainly wasn't going to be my last.

Another consequence of the club closing was that I was now on the outside of the gang house fence. Out there in the world where all the 'other people' existed. With that came more challenges, for example in my own mind I was now on the front line all the time. When I was living at the clubhouse it was easy to relax because you knew you were basically safe inside the fence, but it wasn't like that on the outside. Now it felt like I was on the front line all the time and where previously I had relied on the older guys as a frontline defence, I now had to fill that position. In fact, I was now a front-line representative of what was left of the old club. So, it was even more important now because I was known in a number of circles as 'one of their boys'. I had a reputation to uphold as well as my own personal safety to be concerned about. I could not embarrass the old club and certainly I could not embarrass myself because from my point of view being a man meant that you could not be intimidated, dominated or pushed around. Being a man meant that you were in control! No one else could have power over me otherwise I would be a failure, or at least that's what I believed. Having a girlfriend now also bought with it similar complications because now I not only had to protect the name of the club and myself, but I also had to protect her and not allow any person to tread in my domain, that being anywhere that her domain extended. Very difficult and certainly a lot of responsibility for a young guy who was not even twenty years old yet. Trying to be a dominant, adult male with no weaknesses when I was only nineteen years old put a lot of pressure on me. Perhaps you could say that I didn't necessarily handle that pressure so well.

With this mindset in place, you can perhaps begin to understand the gradual increase in aggression and violence that I succumbed to over time.

Even after the clubhouse was sold, I had this mentality that we were a gang that was not to be messed with. Especially the members and I, but also all our associates and friends. Obviously, there was an informal kind of structure or hierarchy in place where I personally considered ex-members to be the top guys, but then the rest of us had our place too and that circle extended to numerous different area's around Christchurch and beyond to places like Pines Beach, Rangiora and pretty much the wider Canterbury region.

A simple way of explaining how my thoughts constructed themselves in those early days was that I had the personal understanding that a gang or club was a necessity of life and therefor at any cost we must maintain that structure. While the club structure was in place, we enjoyed certain privileges that people outside the club could not enjoy. Privileges such as the club brotherhood or family, loyalty to one another, information or as the parliamentarians call it 'intelligence', belonging, and respect. One factor that was important to me was the ability to mobilise our own security force. As I grew older, I began to think of our crew as our own personal government operating within our own community separate to the rest of the country. Thus, making us the authority over others, the government in the non–policed areas of Canterbury. Which completes the circle and brings us back to the beginning of the necessity of the club's existence. Because if we are our own government then we must be structured and we must have our own security force, just as any country has its own security forces. I shy away from attempting to justify actions that we took over the years but at least by sharing these thoughts I believe people can begin to get an insight into the way a person such as myself has thought in the past. I am also not saying that I was thinking these exact thoughts back in those early years when I was only nineteen, but I do believe that subconsciously some of these beliefs were being acted out. And going back twenty odd years into the nineties and early two thousand's things were different. Meaning that many people didn't rely heavily on police. We had to protect ourselves and from an early age we were always of the understanding that you never involved police in anything. So, without police involvement in our lives, we had to have our own structure in place which for many of us became a gang or club. To add to that you need to understand the landscape of Christchurch during the nineties. Yes, as I have previously stated, Christchurch was a great place to raise a family if you got it right like anywhere else in the world. For those of us whose family had been broken up, or had never been there in the first place, it was often a very different world to the world that others viewed. I saw aggressive and violent people right through my schooling and early teens. When I first started hanging out at the club there were five separate motorcycle clubs in Christchurch. There were also two street gangs, the Black Power and the Mongrel Mob. Among the non-patch wearing groups you found the skin head gangs or the white power gangs. The latter always presented somewhat of an anomaly since a large number of the members were of Māori or Polynesian decent. There were also the youth gangs like the Crips, the Bloods, and then the numerous other factions of different communities that are in fact too many to mention. Finally, it would also be worth mentioning the inner-city night life characters who often saw themselves as gangsters or underworld authorities and ran the brothels and nightclubs. Although many of these groups mentioned were considered by our circle as being on a lower level of the underworld than we were, they were still at times extremely violent, unpredictable and, at the very least, a nuisance at the best of times. Nearly every corner of Canterbury's city and countryside had someone who could present themselves as a problem, whether that be a skinhead, punk, street gang member, club member or even a motely bunch of junkies. There was always somebody and those people needed to be kept at arm's length.

Once you looked closely at what was going on in behind the scenes in Christchurch and began to understand the gravity of the underworld that lay beneath, you perhaps might begin to understand the way we were and why we clung to our club in the way that we did. Yes, obviously many people in the Canterbury region got on with their lives perfectly well without giving a second thought towards issues such as these, but those people were not us. And we were not those people, it just didn't work out that way for us.

Kate my girlfriend, was once the girlfriend of a man named Aaron Howie. Aaron Howie was an associate of the skinhead gang, the Fourth Reich, which had an extremely violent reputation among some communities around the South Island but mainly in Paparoa Prison where the gang originated. As I previously mentioned regarding skinhead gangs, the Fourth Reich also had members that were of Māori decent and as far as I am aware by 1998, Neihana Foster had become the President of the Fourth Reich gang and he was quite obviously a Māori, which I refer to as evidence confirming my earlier comments. In 1997 Aaron Howie and Neihana Foster killed a man in Westport by dragging him across rough terrain, stripping him naked and throwing him into the Buller River where he drowned. According to Kate, Aaron's brother had given evidence against Aaron which contributed to the arrest of both Aaron and Neihana. Aaron and Neihana were later convicted of the crime. I do know that Kate was in contact with Aaron's brother around this period. I also encountered him. One night Aaron's brother was attacked and according to Kate, he turned up at Christchurch hospital with serious injuries. Apparently, he spent two to three weeks in hospital coming in and out of a coma. Family members were reportedly visiting him in hospital after doctors had warned them of the seriousness and uncertainty of the situation. Aaron's brother supposedly told police that he had been walking through town late at night and that he had been attacked by unknown assailants using baseball bats. I am not certain of the veracity of this story, but it is the story that was relayed to me. I have wondered as time went by about the relationship Kate had with Aaron's brother and other scenarios that potentially played out. But without knowing all the facts it is hard to comment much further other than to say this was a very strange storey...

From this point in time forward, things seemed to heat up and speed up. From memory a lot of things happened over a short period of time. I was getting involved with various activities to help out with the money situation. Those activities were loosely based around what some of my friends were doing at the same time. One was growing marijuana and had a small supply which he wanted to sell around town. Another friend was moving anything he could get his hands on, plus manufacturing his own cannabis oil. The oil production was quite low-level stuff that nobody really wanted to get involved with, but it did have its use. Especially when you made a lot of it. Thousands upon thousands of capsules of oil equated to a small income. Likewise, anything you could get your hands on in a large number or quantity of equated to money. This was what a lot of people were doing around Christchurch at the time. Some were supplying the junkie circles with morphine pills and heroin, others just catered to the potheads and the non-junkie circles. Basically, everything that you can imagine that would have been going on probably was, but it was prior to the time of there being a lot of methamphetamines around. During this time speed and meth was not in abundance like it is now. In the circles that I moved in there was a lot of marijuana, LSD and a few different pills going around. That was it, not a huge problem across Christchurch at that time, although I am aware that the junkies always suffered in their addictions going back a long time from probably before I was born. I guess that's why our circle had a no junkies rule and a don't do junk rule. Because it was evil stuff, and most people knew that. In any case we were all up to no good for a while there. Things were brewing and it was about to spill over.

Kate and I were in something of a relationship and we had moved into a house on Brougham Street. We got a border in, who Kate knew through other friends, and I was out doing my activities most of the time. At the time I was spending a lot of time with a friend of mine called Chris. I'd been to school with Chris and subsequently he had come around and visited me outside the clubhouse when it was still there. Chris and I were good friends, and he was a bit like me in a number of ways but of course he was his own person too. Chris was a similar build and height to me with dark hair and a soft face. The girls often liked Chris for his looks, but he was still growing up, so he had yet to master the art of being a man. Chris had a couple of older brothers who were also known around town. The brothers were not bad guys, into their tattooing and generally speaking they had quite a few similar interests to the rest of us, however, they never ended up hanging around as much as Chris did. They were around but only from time to time.

One cold, dark winters night in the middle of Christchurch's Brougham Street, Kate, the border, Chris and I were all at the house enjoying what was left of the evening. All of us were tripping on drugs on this occasion. Things turned a little sour with the border. Kate had been complaining about him prior to that night and, for whatever reason, I can't quite recall exactly, I had a bit of a go at him which led to him taking off in the middle of the night. The border was nearly ten years older than us, a druggy with long hair and a beard. Kate had wanted him there so she could collect a bit of rent of him each week but in the end, he had just turned out to be a nuisance. Later that night as we were starting to come down off the trip, we heard a knock at the door. I went to answer the door and it was a guy by the name of Paul Sutherland. Kate and the border knew this guy and so I let him in, after getting the okay from Kate. This guy was again about ten years older than us and was of medium build and height. He had been around the fringes of a few circles, but I'd never met him before. Like the border, I think he was a bit of a druggy. He came into the lounge where Kate and I sat back down again but this guy Paul remained standing and immediately I sensed something was going on. He had a bit of a smirk on his face and started talking. I don't recall exactly how long he was talking before he said it, and I can't remember what else he said, because the only thing I can remember him saying was "Can I have a go on your girlfriend?"

I presume that what had happened is that our boarder had gone away and complained to some people and that this guy Paul, who knows nothing about who I am or who I'm associated with, decides that he is going to go and involve himself in someone else's disagreement. So basically, he didn't like the border being given a hard time by a couple of teenagers and he's decided to come around to our place and pick a fight. So that's what he did. And here this guy is standing in my lounge looking straight at me asking if he can have sex with my girlfriend.

I have no idea what he was expecting me to do, but I got out of my seat so fast I think I saw the smirk disappear of his face like the lights changing from red to green. Green meant go for him, which is exactly what he did. As soon as he saw me coming towards him, he made straight for the hall-way and the front door. I swooped in behind him without hesitating for a second and in one fluent motion lifted a wooden barstool off the floor until it was over my head and then brought it crashing down on the back of his head just as he was passing through the front door. He had made it to the front door, opened it and then just as he'd nearly passed through to safety, I'd caught him with the full brunt of the stool. I felt the shudder of the impact passing through the legs of the stool and immediately I thought he's done, but then I looked out into the darkness, and he was gone. Nowhere to be found. I was puzzled because I was sure it had been a clean impact, but then I thought afterwards well maybe the guy just had a tough head.

Feeling a little put off by what had just happened we all went back inside and started discussing the situation. The drugs were well and truly wearing off by this stage, which made it a little easier but still I was feeling uneasy. I really didn't like that guy feeling like he had the right to come in here and cause an issue like that. A situation like this reinforces the belief I had regarding the need for a barrier between my crew and the outside world. A deterrent you could say. That deterrent being the existence of an underworld organisation that dealt severely with its adversaries.

Unfortunately, no matter how much of a deterrent you have in place, you will always find people like that who don't necessarily have the highest of IQs and who gain courage through ignorance. So deterrent or no deterrent, situations like this just seem to happen. Little did I know the situation was about to escalate even further. Within an hour or so there was another knock at the door. Chris and I both went to the door this time and when I opened it, I could see Paul Sutherland, apparently now with newly restored armour of courage standing a few metres away from my door with the same smart alec look on his face that he'd had only a few hours previously. I won't take a long time to explain what happened next as otherwise this will end up being a series rather than a book, but it wasn't overly dramatic anyway. Not this part anyway. Basically, Paul came back to the house, knocked, and stood three metres back from the door. I looked outside and saw him standing there and a semi-circle of about ten guys standing a further five metres back from where Paul was standing. Most of the guys standing in support of Paul had a bat or pole on them. Paul started mouthing off and bouncing around on the spot and so I knew it was all on. I evaluated the situation and decided the best way forward was to call him out on his own. This is often a good option. If a man refuses a one-on-one challenge while all his friends are in attendance and there to support him, then the man being called out looks rather pathetic. So that's what I did, as I made my way towards him into the centre of the semi-circle. Immediately we started exchanging a few shots but neither of us really connected. It seemed as if Paul was more interested in bouncing around and mouthing off. Now also remember this, I was only eighteen or nineteen years old. Although I was capable as an ex-rugby player and hunting enthusiast, I still had not fully submerged myself into the heavy-duty fight training and practice that I later took up. I was strong, but I wasn't quite there yet as far as my fighting skills were concerned. Despite this, even though this guy was ten years older than me, there was no way he was going to have any success on this occasion. The worst he was able to do was connect with a couple of light shots to the forehead. That just made me angry and in the blink of an eye, just as I had done inside the house, I lurched towards him in a rage. He sensed it and fled. I chased him all the way down the street and he disappeared into the darkness around the corner again. Now you understand why I questioned this guy's IQ because the reality is that he was a weird one. I walked back to my house past all these guys standing around with bats and poles and stood silently on my front lawn waiting for them to file out and leave which they did. I think most of them were as confused as I was as to what had just happened. Not a word was spoken as they jumped in their vehicles and left.

That was the last I heard of those guys while I lived at that address. Soon after Kate and I shifted to a much nicer house a couple of blocks further up Brougham Street. The new house was warmer, much tidier and had a lot more room, so we were fairly happy to get in there and leave the other old box of a house further up the road. I hadn't forgotten about the incident. It was a breach of my rules as far as I was concerned. The rule states that a person cannot come to my house, either on their own or with a group, and instigate an altercation of any sort. And this was at the serious end of the scale, because there was a group of them. What made it far worse was that this was a family house. Kate had a two-year-old daughter named Pollyanna who anybody who was acquainted with us should have known. I can't recall if Polly was there on the night of the incident, but that was irrelevant because they didn't know if she was there either. Effectively they attacked a family house with children in it. Since I had never met this guy before I knew nothing about him, so I had to find out where Paul lived. It took a while. Finally, Kate came back to me with an area and street name. Apparently, it was the only house on the street which had a big boat parked outside on the front lawn. That was all the information that we needed.

The afternoon we chose to make a move, we had all gathered at my place prior to departing. There was Chris and I plus two other guys who were the same age as us. These two other guys were not included in our club circle. One of them was, in fact, a supporter of the Epitaph Riders Motorcycle Club but we knew them through a female friend of ours. They were available at the time, so we decided they should come along to make up a couple of extra numbers. We drove around to Uncle's house. Remember he was a member of the original club. We talked to Uncle briefly and then he came with us to the address in Shirley. The house was easy to find. I had checked it out prior to that night, so I knew exactly where it was and how we were going to approach the situation. Fairly simple really, through the front door.

Five of us got out of the vehicle and made our way through the cold, dark night towards the front door where we knocked and waited for an answer. It must have been nearing ten o'clock when a guy in his mid-thirties answered the door. I asked him for Paul. He knew straight away something was going on. Out of fear he immediately told us Paul was asleep, before walking towards his room as if to try and wake him up. We knew straight away by his actions that Paul was in that bedroom and within a few seconds we'd pushed in front of the guy and made our way into Paul's bedroom. Paul was asleep under the blankets, as we switched the lights on and pulled the covers off to reveal the target beneath. There was no doubt that it was him. Blond hair and squinting eyes trying to adjust to the light. I attacked him straight away, punching him multiple times in the head. I then jumped up onto the bed and kicked him in the head with my steel toed boot. The boot ricocheted off his head and through the plaster wall behind him. Again, I pulled my leg back and let loose again with the exact same result as the first attempt. Paul's head was absorbing the blows and deflecting the shots into the wall behind him. Three times I connected with his head and the wall behind him which left three perfect holes in the wall a couple of inches apart. As I said previously, this guy must have had a tough head because even after these blows to the head he remained in an upright sitting position on his bed. Blood was trickling down and he was swaying a little, but still in the same position as he was prior to the kicks. I realised we were in a hurry, so I jumped down off the bed and let Chris finish him off. Chris had a full-length machete on him and struck him across the top of both knees and both arms. You could hear the blade hitting the bone on all four occasions and as Chris pulled the machete back from its final strike streams of blood squirted around the room and across the ceiling. It was done and that was the final stage in our judicial process as far as we were concerned.

We filed out of the house, into the car and departed. On our trip back across town I decided I had another job to take care of, so we stopped off at another address in the middle of town where a guy owed me money. I went in with Chris, punched the guy in the head and walked out with his television. He owed me money for a transaction, and he'd obviously decided that he didn't need to pay me. This guy was a junkie and probably thought he could get away with it because he was older than me. Once again in my mind I couldn't let him get away with that, especially because he was an associate of Kate. In a way this had meant that he was giving the message to Kate that he didn't need to worry about her boyfriend. Such a silly little issue I now know but at the time I took it personally.

We made our way back across town, dropping Uncle off on the way. Finally, we pulled up at my place and everyone filed inside. Now this day was about to become a big lesson in my life. I assumed that the guys we had beat up would keep quiet and accept their punishment. I also expected the guys who were with me at the time to behave in an inconspicuous manner that wouldn't bring about any further issues. Both assumptions turned out to be bad assumptions. Within a couple of days police had raided my house.

It was going to be difficult for a while, but I just had to get through this stage of my life and then things would return to normal. On the bright side I had learnt a valuable lesson about police and people. Do not disregard them and do not trust them. To cut a long story short, the two guys that I'd beat up identified us. To add to that, the second of the two extras, who we had taken along with us, stole property from the first house and then was kind enough to leave the property at my place to be found by police. When I think back now it was just so ridiculous, but I guess when you're young and full of energy you just don't think about these things. The guy in question, who stole the property and left it at my house, was not the Riders supporter but the second one, the friend of the Riders supporter. All he took from the property was a small clock and a stack of CDs but that was enough to get me done for robbery. That really annoyed me too, because the last thing I was is a thief. Even my mother would vouch for me on that one. All of us were arrested, apart from Uncle who Paul Sutherland had conveniently been unable to identify.

We were booked on a raft of charges. After some time on remand, we were advised by our lawyers to go with a plea bargain and plead guilty to lesser charges. Initially I was charged with aggravated robbery times two and grievous bodily harm times two but, after our lawyers put together the deal, my charges were dropped to robbery, theft and injuring. The police identified me as the ringleader and so put the more serious charges on me, however, Chris took full responsibility for the machete attack which took a big load off my plate. The two extra guys were given even smaller charges than Chris and me. In the end, I think we all served around about the same amount of time, except for Chris who served the longest. The reason for the judge's leniency on me was because I made a big effort as we were approaching sentencing, with a lot of support from my mother and her church associates. You need to do that sometimes; I know a lot of people will say screw the system, but the reality is you're better off to try and show the sentencing judge that you do feel some remorse and that you won't do it again. It's as simple as that really. I think I wrote my own letter to the judge. Not a huge deal, but enough for him to decide to give me the break I needed to be out within a year. Another ticket I had on my side was that I knew the probation officer who wrote my probation report. His daughter was my girlfriend in primary school, and I'd remained her friend through-out the early years of high school as well. So he knew me. That was just a bit of luck though, nothing untoward going on there.

By the grace of the Almighty One I was given twelve months in prison. Automatic half because it wasn't longer than a year. The judge obviously liked me as well and that, coupled with my age, meant he didn't want my future destroyed inside a prison block. It wasn't going to be easy though, and this would be the beginning of a long-term process that would take many a winding turn.

CHAPTER 9
FIGHTING FOREVER

The year was 1997. At the age of nineteen I still looked, in my opinion like a little guy, maybe average if you were being generous. So, as I headed into prison for the first time, it was obvious that there would be some significant challenges coming my way. However, despite my own shortcomings it appeared as though I had luck on my side. Or, from the perspective of my mother and the people on the outside who were praying for me, a very powerful God was on my side. Some might ask how God could be looking after a wicked person like me, which is a good question, but I guess the answer is that He sees the big picture rather than the small picture. Or simply put, He had His reasons.

We first entered the prison system after the initial arrest. We were held in the police cells for a few nights and then transferred to Addington Remand Prison where nearly all the remand prisoners were housed. There was a small pre-release unit over the back but that wasn't really a part of the main Addington prison. The main block at Addington was about the size of an average school gym. This was an old-style prison with none of the luxuries that the new modern blocks have like showers in your cells. All we had was a bucket and if you wanted a shower you had to walk the platform down to the shower block and take a shower where everyone else did. It was cold, boring, and for a few hours each day you'd get let outside into the yard. I'll briefly mention a few of the people in there and the main events that took place. There were some people in there who were okay and some bad. I know there was a Road Knight member in there for murder at the time and there was also a Tribesmen member from up North, who I believe was serving time for manslaughter. There was another Tongan guy who'd been in and out of prison for half his life and it was mostly for rape I think. The world is made up of all types. The guys charged and convicted in the Caledonian Hotel murder were also in there at the same time as us, because at that stage they hadn't been convicted and were still on remand. The ones who were in Addington with us were Levi Rushton, Patterson Tekura, and Daniel Pou. As far as I am aware Richard Tuhora was being housed up North during this time. These guys were part of the Crips gang. They had robbed a bottle store and shot the bartender in the process and now they were all awaiting trial, some on murder charges and others on lesser charges of robbery. There were obviously a lot of other guys in there too but we had no contact with many of them. The only time you really had contact with other inmates was when you'd be heading down the stairs for a meal or when you'd be going out to the yard for exercise. Chris and I were celled up together. You could have very short conversations with others coming and going as you moved around the block or spoke to someone through the bars, but the only time you really got to spend a significant amount of time with other prisoners was when you went to the yard.

We were assigned to the youth yard, because we were under twenty. It was reasonably relaxed, and we didn't have a lot to worry about while we were in there but the small amount of activity that did take place happened in the yard. The first event was when Patterson Tekura tried to throw a shot at me through the bars. They were walking past our yard and we were against the bars, when I presume he thought he had an opportunity to stand over us because we were younger. When I laughed at his suggestion, he tried to fire one at me. It was a failed attempt and they just kept on walking past. That was not long after we first got in there and I guess it was just his way of figuring out who we were. The next guy to cause a stir was David Lei. David was a really big Tongan guy who was a trained boxer. His father was a boxer and I have no doubt that David really knew how to fight as well. Funnily enough it never came to that. When he first came into the yard Chris and I had been thinking we might have to stab this guy because he was an obvious threat. We had already put plans in place to do just that, but as soon as we met him, we realised he was for us and not against us. He wanted to be our friend and I didn't mind David. In recent years I heard some bad rumours from another guy we were in there with, but it's not my business so I'll just take him for the person he was when he was a young fella and that wasn't too bad.

The Crips seemed to be the ones in there that had a problem with us initially. Daniel Pou, who was the one who pulled the trigger at the Caledonian Hotel was constantly staring at me and it wouldn't be long before he was put in a yard with us because of his age. I can't remember the exact timing of when this happened but I'm sure David Lei got put in the yard with Pou before he was put in with us. In any case, apparently all you could hear coming from their yard was thump, thump, "ahhhh!, ahhhh!". Patterson in the next yard over couldn't see what was going on because of the block wall. He thought it was David Lei beating me up, but obviously it wasn't me because I'm not even sure if I was there that day. Possibly I was in court or had a visitor, but really what was going on was David was beating up Pou. David thumped him around and jumped on his head before the guards ordered him out of the yard. I'm pretty sure it was either the next day or not long after that David was put in with us.

Some time went by before we heard that Pou was going to be put in with us. The tension was rising before he came in. I was a little surprised when he challenged me to a fight on the first day out in the yard. David wasn't there that particular day so it may have just been Chris, me and a couple of other guys.

Once the guards had moved around the other side of the tower and could no longer be seen Pou challenged me. He said, "Let's go then."

We came together in the middle of the yard and Pou threw a couple of strange looking punches at me. They reminded me of a cricket bowl, but they were completely ineffective, so I just laid into him with a bunch of straight ones. Pou curled up on the ground within about ten seconds and I gave him a couple of extra ones while he was down there, before the guard looked down at me from the tower and asked me if I had finished which I had. I walked off and that was that.

Chris and I came to blows one day as we were walking down the stairs to get our breakfast. We'd been celled up together for ages and this particular day we were arguing. I cannot remember what was said but Chris hit me from behind with a plastic jug. I barely felt the impact of the jug because it was just plastic but the action just caused us to erupt into a full-blown brawl in the middle of the stairs which the guards almost immediately stopped. They separated us and put us in the two lock up cells side by side on the bottom landing while they decided what to do with us. I told Chris I wanted a one-on-one straight away out in the yard, but Chris was not into that idea. Over the course of the next few days he opted to accept a free shot in the face next opportunity we got out the yard. So, I laid a good one on him out in the yard hoping it would leave a mark on his face, and after that we were back to being friends again.

Not long before our sentencing and move to Paparoa Prison, the guards were moving me around out the front one day. They were about to put me in a cell with Rushton and Patterson, when just at the last minute the guard said "Oh, you don't want to go in there do you?"

He obviously realised what he was doing and gave me the option of going elsewhere. I just looked at him straight away and said, "Put me in there, I'm fine".

So, the guard shut the door behind me, locked it and walked across the hallway to the guard's office. To my surprise Patterson and Rushton were both pleasant. They asked me how I was and there was a little more small talk and that was it. Sometimes with guys like that they appreciate a person that stands his ground. I'm positive that's what went on that particular day. They knew I was uncomfortable in there with them, but they valued the fact that I had the balls to do it.

After sentencing I was shipped over to Paparoa Prison. Upon arriving at Paparoa they informed me that the centre wing where you are first supposed to go upon arrival was full. There were only two options left: West Wing (protection), or East Wing where all the lifers and long termers go. Most of the murderers and anyone with a serious long-term conviction would end up in East. There was no way I was going to protection, so I immediately told them they'd have to put me in East which is what they did. East was a large facility with a lot of cells. I actually thought it was better than Addington though in spite of the fact that there were a lot of dangerous prisoners in there. Firstly, you had your own cell with a proper toilet and wash basin. It definitely had a more of a modern feel to it than Addington. This is where I was first able to hang a cotton thread from the ceiling and it became my first improvised boxing bag. This was a few metres long and dangled from the roof down to waist height. Although it gave no resistance to my punches, it did give me a target. Effectively I was shadow boxing.

Outside there were a number of yards where people went for their outside activities. There was the white boy yard which had all the white boys, skins, a few Road Knight supporters and the like. Then there was the Black Power. Finally, there was the neutrals yard which contained a mixture of everybody and a few old Mongrel Mob members. The Mongrel Mob was fairly small in the South Island during those years, so there were only a few incarcerated when I was there.

I was only supposed to be in East Wing until a spot opened for me in the Centre Wing, but while I was there I wasn't concerned at all about the environment. Only as concerned as I imagine any normal person would be when put into a hostile environment such as this, so when the opportunity came up for me to go out to the yard I went straight out. Of course, I went out to the white boy's yard, however, I'm not sure if I was invited out there or if I chose that yard for some other reason. Gary Wilson was one of the prisoners in the white boys' yard. He was somehow related to the Harris's or the Knights or one of those groups. I'm not exactly sure where he stood but I would put him on that side because he wasn't with my old club. Nor was he with the Henchmen, Riders, Handlebars Club or either of the street gangs. Basically, I think he was a big, musclebound skinhead who leaned towards that other side most of the time. Another guy was named Chippy. He apparently later killed himself for reasons only known to those close to him. The third guy I will refer to had a ginger- head with skinheads tattooed across the back of it. The three of them were several years older than me and were all aligned in one way or another to the same group. The other side. Anyway, Gary came over and started talking to me and asked who I was and so forth, obviously trying to work out which side I was on. I immediately told him I was associated with the club. He then asked me about one of the extras that we'd taken along with us on the night we'd done our attack and I confirmed that yes, he was our co-offender. The problem was that this extra guy was an Epitaph Riders supporter. His nickname was Dirty, and he and his brother were friends with the Suttons who were all tied in with the Riders. This didn't really mean much to me because I had personally never had anything to do with the Riders. What I did not realize was that Gary obviously had a problem with it and he decided to act on it.

Without making a big deal about it and, to hide his concern, Gary then changed the subject before casually asking if I'd like to have a puff of marijuana with him and his mates. I happily accepted the offer and followed them into the covered bathroom area which was out of sight from the guards' viewing platform. Gary, me, Chippy and the guy with skinheads tattooed on the back of his head all filed into this bathroom area where I was expecting a nice smoke. Suddenly in the far corner of the bathroom, Gary Wilson turned on me and started throwing punches. Pausing for a second here, think about my earlier statement from the start of the chapter about the people on the outside who were praying that the all-powerful God would look after me. The mysterious Almighty, nobody knows exactly what He does, what His work is and what it isn't. They will say they know but how can anyone know all things unless they are Him?

Gary had just thrown his first couple of punches at me while Chippy and the other guy were waiting for their opportunity to put in their work as well. These guys were all big guys, Gary being the biggest at probably thirty or forty kilograms heavier than me. Chippy was also a bigger man than me and the ginger headed guy was also tall and wiry. They had it over me in age, experience, height, weight and, to add to that, it was three on one. Surely, I was done. The speed in which this took place was equivalent to a few blinks of the eye. And in that amount of time I ducked under Gary's punches, tackled him backwards into the urinal where he lost his balance and forward motion, before I turned my attention on the other two that were trying to grab me from behind. I spun around until I was facing them, then headfirst ploughed into the two of them leaving Gary behind me petering on the edge of the wetback urinal. The two in front of me bounced out of my way as I took large strides to move out from underneath the cover of the bathroom block and away from their failed attack.

Standing out from under the covered area and looking back at where I had just come from, I could see an extremely irritated Gary Wilson looking out from within the shadows. From above the guards yelled down at me to come out of the yard. They must have seen me exit the covered area and realised something had just happened. I refused to leave the yard at first, but the guards yelled back that if I didn't come out, they'd drag me out. Locked up again in my cell for the next three days, the guards refused to let me out. Soon after they moved me into Centre North for the transitional stage of my vacation.

Centre North and more action on the way. It was an old and dirty prison and there was no way out. I stayed in Centre North for a few weeks, or maybe a month or two, I can't exactly remember, but I stayed there until I was shifted to the pre-release unit at Addington. While in Centre North, on my way back from lunch one day Chris and I were walking alongside the yard which contained a few Homeys in it. Just as we were moving past Reece Skipper, another guy on our side of the bars stalled in front of us and turned around. I knew something was up straight away, so I passed my bread roll and cup of tea to Chris to hold on to while I dealt with this guy who appeared to have some sort of problem with me. Reece and one of his accomplices put their arms through the bars and tried to grab hold of me while the guy on my side of the bars attacked me. Reece and his mates were the same age as me, while the guy who attacked me from my side was at least ten years older than me with a reasonably muscly physique. It's hard to understand precisely what the issue was here, but I didn't really care. Just more of the same, wasn't it? People want to fight. Reece and his friend had no power to hold me, so I immediately slipped out of their grasp and as the guy on my side threw his lazy hook at me, I simply avoided it and smacked him straight in the mouth before he even knew what hit him. Blood trickled down his startled face and he swiftly backpedalled away from us. He now knew it had been a bad idea and realised his best option was to move away without any further incident.

Later that day the guys in the wing were laughing at this older fella because he'd had his lip split open by a teenager. I guess it is a little comical, but it could have easily gone the other way so really, it's not that funny. I should be thankful that these situations didn't turn out worse for me because I know for a fact not everyone gets through as easily as I did. By the way, Chris was still holding my bread roll and cup of tea by the time I finished with that guy. In hindsight I thought that was strange. Over time I learnt that Chris was not always there. A similar event had occurred at the district courts one day when I fought with these two skinheads only to turn around and find Chris just standing there watching me. At times he was good but other times he just wasn't with it, and I just had to appreciate him for when he was there.

I was soon to be moved out of Centre North and over to Addington pre-release. As I said previously any prison sentence that was twelve months or less was automatically halved so my twelve-month sentence was actually only six months. I'd done three months on remand at Addington right at the beginning and from then on things were moving fairly quickly. There were only a couple of incidents that occurred while in Addington, but neither were serious. In one instance there, an inmate had been stealing or "tea leafing" as it's called from around the unit, so my cell mate and I set a trap for him using actual tea leaves. We filled an empty tobacco pouch with tea leaves and left it in plain sight of the hallway. Of course, it went missing quite quickly and he was found with it in his room. He was a short, stocky

Islander who was about the same age as me. Unfortunately for him he did not know how to fight so when I came up against him, I was quickly able to outmanoeuvre him and sit him on the ground where I let rip with a number of blows. The guy was lucky because, had the fight not been stopped, I was only a matter of seconds away from hitting him with a wooden ashtray that I had just managed to lay my hands on. Yes, this is bad, and I wasn't always a very pleasant person but that was the life at this stage. I hadn't yet worked out a better way. I'd been trained in one simple method of justice, so I followed it.

The next incident involved a guy with dreadlocks who had just got off the phone in a really bad mood. He'd nudged past me on his way down the hall. I took exception because it was obvious he'd done it on purpose. We agreed to a one-on-one fight in the common room, where we ended up in a full-on grappling wrestle. Nobody got hurt and it was even from start to finish. The guy was again a good ten years older than me, and it gave me a bit of a reminder that we needed to be prepared for the unexpected. Here I had been practicing upright shadow boxing and, before I knew it, I was involved in a fight on the ground with somebody equally as strong as me. That was a good reminder.

I don't know the exact date of my release, but I do know I was still nineteen. Prior to my release I had been allowed out on a couple of different occasions. This included a day parole to visit home where Kate still lived, and I believe that I also had day paroles for study purposes. Whatever the number of outings was it can't have been significant because overall it was a fairly short sentence which meant my pre-release period was also short.

I was out though, and thankful that it was all over. Not long after I got out, I broke up with Kate. I lost interest in her for a few reasons, one of them being the fact that there were other women out there who I decided were better women than Kate. I didn't trust her. Kate was an alcoholic, into drugs and I don't think she knew how to be the type of woman I needed in my future. That was that, done. At some stage she moved out of the house, and I hardly had anything to do with her after that.

Over the years the fights would continue and become more and more frequent. The time in prison was just a taster and only encouraged me to train at a higher level. For now, I was about to focus on some different activities. Activities that certainly wouldn't draw me any closer to the light at the end of the tunnel but rather would draw me closer into the darkness.

CHAPTER 10

DARKNESS

Back in Christchurch after my release from prison I had no problems settling into my old, but at the same time, new routine. A lot can change in such a short space of time and that was certainly the case in this instance. New accommodation, new people on the scene, and a slightly different feel about where we were heading in the future. I visited a lot of my old friends and caught up on what was going on and what people were thinking about doing. The younger guys wanted a club again and so we rented a big, old house down on Hoon Hay Road which we converted into our new clubhouse. The walls were painted black, a bar was built, doors fortified, and other renovations were constantly on the go. It was a good setup as a starting point and for the first few weeks we had some great parties. I had my twentieth birthday there with a lot of the original members from the club turning up. Uncle was there, Dougal, the sergeant-at-Arms, and several others. It was great to see Shorty and Rick again. There was a lot of alcohol and a lot of good times during that short period of time when everything was running smoothly. Some of the new guys who were hanging around were quite good guys too. It was all going well but how long would that last?

As time went by fights, incidents and significant events became so many in number and so frequent that it would be impossible to remember every incident. To give explanations and details about everything that ever happened would be a never-ending process.

A gang known as the Back Yard Boozers sprung up in Christchurch that was mainly comprised of European guys in their early twenties. We had previously had some contact with them and on one occasion they had behaved in a borderline manner which brought into question their level of respect for us and their future motives. There had been a one-on-one fight arranged between me and one of their members. According to our code this should have been a respectful and simple process, but upon arrival at the predetermined address the member who was supposed to be there to resolve the issue was missing. Instead, two other members of the Boozers who were known to us were walking around in the house with bats. They did not become aggressive or make any threats, but the fact that they had bats in their possession and the way they were interacting with us indicated that there was some sort of problem. We left on that occasion without any further incident, expecting something to happen in the future.

A period of time passed and a guy by the name of Shane who had been there on this previous occasion rang me. He had a problem with me because I had said something to my ex-girlfriend about him that he was not happy about. Apparently, I had implicated him in a situation with another girl which had caused a problem between him and his girlfriend. He yelled down the phone at me, "You're going over," before hanging up the phone.

According to reports, not long after this three people entered his house via the front door and attacked him and a fellow Boozer member with fists and a bat. Some were saying that I was one of the perpetrators, although no complaint was ever made to police.

On another occasion after this event was reported to have happened, two carloads of Back Yard Boozers were said to have been traveling down Hoon Hay Road. According to reports they parked their cars at one prearranged meeting point and then proceeded on foot. Shortly after this, assailants converged on the procession of Back Yard Boozers and an exchange of gunfire was heard up and down the street. Police reports indicated that thirteen shots were fired, and that two Back Yard Boozers were hospitalised with gunshot wounds.

Police immediately began a major investigation, and the following morning raided our clubhouse on Hoon Hay Road. Several of us were arrested and charged with possession of explosives because police had found Molotov cocktails at our address. No one was charged in relation to the previous night's shooting although police held several of us in custody over the explosives and questioned us extensively regarding the incident in question. Police suggested that we were the ones who had been involved with the shooting. There were rumours circulating that I had in fact been the one that had pulled the trigger, but no evidence was ever presented.

During the early stages of us setting up the Hoon Hay clubhouse we were having meetings and had our own crew running with those we considered members and those that were considered supporters or associates. I always thought it was a little cheap or childish to give ourselves a club name, so we resisted the temptation to do so and maintained the structure without any title. The media and news outlets however took the name of the old original club and effectively called us the young version of that club. This was outside of our control and to this day we still do not know who told them of the connection between us and the old club. It meant that the entire Hoon Hay Road incident was on the six o'clock news and throughout the major papers. Initially the news suggested it was a war between

Road Knights and Epitaph Riders, but shortly afterwards they corrected themselves and stated that it was nothing to do with Knights and Riders.

By this stage I and two other members had been remanded in custody without bail. The rest of the guys, who had not been arrested all became immediately uncomfortable with the heavy police presence and surveillance. A fire had broken out at the rented clubhouse almost straight after the police search teams had finished there. Nobody knows how the fire started and I do not recall there ever being any conclusion from the fire department as to what actually happened. The end result was that we abandoned the property and plans were made to set up elsewhere. Considering the amount of heat and limelight that was being shone on us at this particular point in time, it probably wasn't such a bad thing.

We used a friend's house on Madras Street for a short period of time but none of us really liked this because he was living there with his girlfriend. Around this time several of the older members from the original club came on board. The sergeant-at-arms, Miller, Uncle, and Rick the prospect all wanted to be involved. This was good for us because it meant an immediate jump in numbers and strength. A couple of the old supporters also came on board and since they were older, experienced guys, they were soon promoted to membership status. By this stage there was a good mix of original members, prospects, and supporters plus all the new, young guys and children of the original members. We were set as long as we could manage our affairs correctly.

The next move was to rent a large warehouse over in Hornby on Waterloo Road. I had been bailed by this stage and so was able to play a part in this move. It really was a great set up because it was a massive, square, red brick building that was totally enclosed with the exception of the gate at the front. The outside wall created the perimeter of the property and then all the rooms including the one which would become our bar area were along the inside of the exterior wall, with a sizeable courtyard in the middle. It was a bit like our own wee castle. The outside wall would have been at least ten foot tall. Really it was perfect. Just a pity we didn't own it. A lot of parties were had at this new property and things moved along quickly. Most of us had bikes and so we were also out on regular rides. I'd picked up a mint 1991 Harley Davidson 1200 Sportster and sold my Triumph Bonneville to another one of the guys. The rest of the boys who didn't have a bike were fast on their way to getting one.

What happened from this moment forward was a blur of hard drugs, rides, fights and worse. I can basically remember what happened over the course of the next few years but obviously it was a long time ago and due to the lifestyle we were living at the time, sometimes I have struggled to remember not so much what happened but in what order it happened. I do know for the second time in my life I was given methamphetamine and from that moment forward we had a lot of it. Meth would eventually become the worst poison that would ever enter the underworld in New Zealand, and across the rest of the world for that matter, but as a first-hand witness to New Zealand's epidemic I can say it was extremely bad here. Meth is a killer and should be exterminated from within our society. If the leaders of this nation put as much emphasis on exterminating meth-amphetamine as they did on eliminating Covid 19 for example, then you would probably save as many lives and save the country literally billions of dollars in social programs and rehabilitation. But anyway, that's a story for a different day. At that time we were on it and we would be going hard for some time. But obviously it wasn't just for the sake of indulgence. There was money in meth which played a massive part in the seduction of so many people.

GANGLAND TO GUINEA

In hindsight we would have been better off if none of us had ever had anything to do with it but unfortunately that wasn't to be the case. Our lives moved forward under the shadow of meth.

Under the shadow of the drug and under the shadow of darkness. That is where we lived. I had been training a lot on the boxing bag and often I would be found preparing myself for the inevitable fights that would soon be coming our way. I was getting a lot better, and with speed on my side I was able to throw twenty punches in half as many seconds. Fast, straight and accurate. When sparring with friends or generally just playing around, I could tell the other guys were completely outmatched and I began to realise I had some special talent for this. I grew in confidence and my speed, coupled with the strength and stamina I'd gained as a young fella through hunting and farming, prepared me for the times ahead. And this is really when the serious fighting began. From here on in the fights would be coming in so frequently I would completely lose count of the number of each and every fight. I was winning that's all I know, but literally there were so many that I can't even remember them all.

One time I tried to estimate roughly how many I had had and the figure was about seventy, but in all likelihood there was more. Especially if you take into account the fights I had from when I was first hanging around the club at fourteen years old. There were a couple of fights I had at our club with the prospect, Shorty, and one of the supporters. Then at least a few before I went into prison and a minimum of six in prison. After being released from prison, I can remember another couple of fights, one of them being with a new recruit that I beat up after he attacked some of our visitors and then turned on us. He was a bit of a bad guy that fella who we were happy to see go. Moving on from that era until we were on Waterloo Road more action took place.

One of our new recruits, who I'll call Baker, was brought in by one of the old original members. He'd already had a bit of experience in prison and on the outer, so he was a frontline asset to have. I became great friends with Baker and the two of us spent a lot of time in the central city visiting the clubs and some of the strip clubs together. We had a lot in common and both of us wanted to see the resurrection of the original club and the expansion of our underworld regime. At one time I stopped to think about the incidents Baker and I had had in town, and I believe for fifteen weeks in a row we had been in town together and been involved in a fight each time. Not only that but we had won every single one of them. There were some serious ones too, with some capable fighters like the Golden Gloves boxer on Armagh Street who I had dealt with in a matter of seconds. Not surprisingly a month or so later I ran into him again at a different bar in town when my friend came to me for assistance. I was drinking at the bar and my friend came and told me how this big guy was in the toilets mouthing off. He wanted me to accompany him to the toilets to sort him out. As soon as I got in there, I realised it was the same guy, only for some reason this time he looked a lot bigger than last time. We immediately started fighting but I was far too quick for him. I got inside his defence within a second or too and pummelled him until he bent over in an attempt to cover up which gave me the opportunity to drop my weight onto his back and force him down to the ground. He ended up on his hands and knees with my knees in the perfect position to finish him off, but at that very second the bouncer came in which brought the proceedings to a halt. Another time at one of the strip clubs a trained kick boxer had a go at me. He was at least six foot four inches and solid but, yet again, I finished him off in only a few seconds. Most of the fights were very fast. The reality was that if you hadn't finished them off in the first ten seconds then you may have had a problem on your hands. That was how you won, lighting fast, launch your attack and connect before they had any opportunity to get their attack underway. If they were able to get even half their attack underway then obviously you could be injured. So don't give them the chance. That's how I did it.

Moving on from my escapades with Baker in town, and out into the suburbs and other places where the fights and incidents continued. One time I was driving out of town towards Brighton in my station wagon when I saw Richie McMillan, the president of the Back Yard Boozers, driving into town in one of his cars. As soon as I saw him, I pulled over and did a U-turn and doubled back. By now Richie had come to a standstill and was waiting to turn right into a side street. I came up from behind him and drove straight into his passenger side door pushing them right across the other side of the road and nearly bending his car into the shape of a banana. I watched as his passenger started freaking out, his body pressed up against the car window as the car was pushed right across the road. I came to a standstill and watched as Richie's car bunny hopped its way down the road in a desperate attempt to get away. Suddenly flashing blue and red lights were upon us and the sound of a police siren forced me over to the side of the road where I parked my station wagon. I jumped out straight away to be greeted by plain clothed cops. It was an undercover police car which explains why I hadn't seen them leading up to the accident. I was totally calm and told them "Look it was an accident, I didn't mean to do that, and my foot simply slipped off the clutch".

The cops obviously realised there was more to the storey than what I had just told them, but they seemed far more interested in chasing Richie than investigating me. I was fine with that. They quickly jumped into their car and sped after him. Perhaps they wanted to get him for leaving the scene of an accident. I never heard another word about that incident. As soon as the police left the scene, I assumed I was within my rights to leave. I drove the nearly unusable wagon over to Waterloo Road and parked it in its final resting place outside the castle. Baker and I also had a run in with Richie and a few of his guys at a sport's bar on Church Corner, Riccarton Road. Well actually it was just back from Church Corner in the car park of the Bush Inn Centre. Richie and I stood face to face and exchanged blows for a few seconds before I looked around and saw that Baker had clean knocked out both of Richie's accomplices. Richie backpedalled quickly, as others tried to drag his friends into waiting cars. It was over as soon as everyone noticed what Baker had done.

There were so many of these little incidents going on all the time that now as I sit here remembering them all I'll remember a few and then forget them again and then remember some other ones and then forget those ones until I think about the area again. It seems as though if I think of a setting then the fights will come back to me and then if I think of another setting, I'll remember more fights that we had in that area. Rangiora is a good example, just as I'm sitting here thinking of Rangiora three different fights come to mind that took place in that area, plus another in Pines Beach which is ten minutes from Rangiora. And another in Belfast right by the old president's house. The first one I remembered from Rangiora was at a bar on the main street. The guy was up at the bar talking to me and for no reason at all he just deliberately insulted me as if I meant nothing to him. It was his way of attempting to dominate me, so I struck him three times in the jaw with my right before he even knew what had happened. He crumpled to the floor in a heap knocked out cold. His friends came over to help him out, but they soon realised they were outnumbered and took it no further. Matt Flintock also turned up at a party in Rangiora one night and tried to start a fight with me so I dealt with him in about five seconds with about ten punches. He was a big guy too and was known for trying to pick on people, but this particular night he tried to pick on the wrong guy. The third fight I remember from Rangiora was at a friend's house on the outskirts where I believe our female friend was having her 21st birthday party. Her cousin had come up from down South and apparently, he was a trained boxer. Baker had just thrown a few punches at the boxer's friend. As soon as Dougal, the old original club member, saw something was going on he yelled out for a one-on-one, which somehow I was immediately tied into. I'm not even sure if I knew anything was going on prior to this happening other than perhaps this boxer guy had been making fun of my hair because at this time it was a bit of a mop. I learnt that he'd been mocking my hair style just as I was getting roped into this fight.

So I was a little bit cheesed off at Dougal for roping me into this fight right in front of everyone else, but I could hardly avoid it at this stage because I had about twenty people standing there watching me. The guy came flying towards me obviously trying to grapple me instead of having a box with me. I swiftly gouged him in the eye which opened him up for a few seconds and then I came up with a solid upper cut that dropped him to the ground before I gave him a boot to the head to finish him off. I wasn't interested in any long-drawn-out fight. I just wanted him out of my way so I could get back to relaxing as I was before he came up to me. He was the classic example of a trouble making, aggressive young guy that picked on me for no reason and subsequently paid the price.

The fight in Pines Beach that I mentioned was with a guy who owed money. I'd rung him to try and arrange a time to sort it out. He'd hurled abuse down the phone at me and threatened me with another club. Uncle and I went out there and found him in a sleepout where a fight ensued. I hooked him multiple times in the head causing him to lose a fair amount of blood. He wasn't a very nice guy and he'd put me in a bit of a position by threatening me on the phone in a way I then felt obligated to respond. The Belfast fight was just another one on a different day whereby a half-drunk guy had insulted the old president in a pub which had subsequently led to a fight outside. The president had already had a go with him, but I ended up getting involved as well. Fight after fight, when would it stop? On New Year's Eve one year all of us were at the Dux de Lux in town. It was really busy and the bar inside was so full you could hardly move. I'd seen this guy before; a big solid six-footer who was a known fighter. On this occasion he was obviously high on something barging his way through the crowd bouncing people out of his way. There was no way he was going to do that to me I thought. As soon as he was within arm's reach of me, I put my hand out to warn him he'd come far enough and that he wasn't going to push me out of his way like he'd just done to everyone else. No surprise, the guy kept lunging forward and not only that but he started throwing haymakers at me. I got in awfully close and pulled myself up to his neck as if I was on a climbing wall and then head locked him before putting extreme pressure on his neck. I felt the neck click and his body went limp. That was it. He was down and out on the ground. Keep in mind this guy may have nearly weighed twice as much as me; he was a dangerous guy.

There was the Blues Bar fight where I took a guy that was about six foot four inches down to the ground by his head in about two seconds. I wrenched him over like I was pulling a sack off the back of a truck. He was a big solid guy too, so I'm guessing he could have been dangerous. Another time our young friend Paddy was attacked one night at a house where he'd ended up sleeping over after some drinks. Some young guys weighed into him with steel bars and Paddy was covered with bruises. I was called in to sort the issue out. We went to the house and gave this guy the option of choosing who he wanted to have a one–on–one with. He picked me, obviously because he had no idea who I was but also because he would have seen my baby face look and decided I was the easiest one. It did not work out well for him and I'm not exactly sure how he was afterwards, but I heard he wasn't doing well. I can justify what I was doing with statements about self-defence and self-determination and so forth, but I personally believe something else was going on here. Is this not darkness? Is this not living in a place of darkness? Always on edge, fortifying our homes and properties to repel attacks, possessing illegal weapons out of fear that they would be needed, and living with a siege mentality all the time. What about the spiritual realm? If this fighting was purely for a just cause and was carried out by righteous men, then perhaps you could say you were still living in the light, but my personal conviction is that we were well outside the bounds of a just cause. We were most definitely living in the realm of darkness.

CHAPTER 11

DARKNESS II

In the last chapter I referred to roughly thirty-seven fights and that's only some of them. Yes, it was a dark place that we lived, and it would only get worse, but I can tell you now, that at this stage of the journey a revelation was only just around the corner. Although the turnaround would take a significant amount of time, the trigger for that reversal was about to happen.

Also keep in mind the fights I referred to in the previous chapter were at different stages of my life. They did not all happen in the same year or even three years. These were different events from different periods of time, but I do know that a lot of these incidents were in the early stages simply by considering who was with me when a certain event happened. For example, if Baker was with me, I know I was in my early twenties and likewise if my young friend Rob was with me, I know it was probably late twenties to early thirties. So that's one way I can work it out, but for now let's move back to the setting of the Waterloo Road rental clubhouse which we eventually had to vacate because the landlord suddenly decided to sell the property.

At this stage I think we were still on bail or remand for the explosives' charges. To bring that part of the storey to an end, we three accused went to trial for these charges. The prosecution stated that we had the Molotov cocktails in our possession at the address on Hoon Hay Road, while our defence lawyers argued that they had been left there by unknown persons attempting to attack the property. The evidence put forward by the defence was that the Molotov cocktails were in an area that was not accessible to the occupants of the house due to the doors of the house being permanently closed. The Molotov cocktails were reported by police to have been found on a veranda outside the house near some shrubbery and trees which our defence lawyers argued was consistent with the theory that unknown assailants had placed them there either for the purpose of using them later or during the process of an unsuccessful attack. Our defence suggested that if these explosives belonged to the occupants of the house, then they would have been placed somewhere accessible, which was not the case.

In the end it was a hung jury, which meant we had to go to a retrial. I cannot remember if we actually went to the second trial or if it was called off prior to the sitting, but the final result was that the charges were dismissed due to the lack of a conviction.

Following that, we moved out of the Waterloo Road property and started having meetings at Millers own house on the other side of town. He had a bar and the property was fortified, so it wasn't a bad set up for the time being. The problem on the horizon were silly insignificant incidents which led to bigger difficulties. I will try not to waste a lot of time here but my reference to these issues will give some insight into the overall timeline. Prior to our move away from Waterloo Road, some of the guys had started to moan and grumble about each other. We had a disagreement involving Uncle, Rick and a couple of the other guys which resulted in Uncle being reprimanded. From that time forward he had a chip on his shoulder towards the rest of us. I would have considered these problems to be insignificant, but as is typical with human nature, a lot of people don't like things being resolved easily and we began squabbling.

There was another matter that increased tension. Apparently, after we had moved out of the Waterloo property some possessions were left there that later went missing. I recall a number of people being accused of this theft. During a conversation with Miller and another close friend of ours, Miller made the statement that Uncle had probably been the one who took the reportedly missing items. I was angry about this because we were supposed to be a united front and here you have one original member of the club, Miller, accusing Uncle of theft in front of a person that was not yet a member. It just looked sloppy. I didn't like it. When I look back on this incident now and recall some other pieces of evidence, I believe that the deceitfulness of human nature began to work its way through our friendships and started to pull us down. Little cracks began to appear and wedges formed between all of us.

It was a real shame because we had some good times while we were meeting over at Miller's house and even before that. The problem was that now some of us were breaking our own rules. Something had to be done, so the next time there was a meeting at Miller's house I let rip on him. He came back at me, but it was a simple manoeuvre to whip his legs out and have him flat on his back and subdued. I was dominant and that was obvious to all those who were present. Yes, you could say I too had broken the rules by letting him have it. My philosophy was that if I didn't do it, then it's not going to be done by anyone else, so it needed to be done which it was. Miller wasn't happy about it and so within a couple of weeks he pulled the pin and opted out of the club. It was done and dusted and within a short period of time we moved meetings over to another member's house which was also fortified and set up with a bar and party area.

We were not wearing gang patches at this time. Firstly, we had decided to not name our crew. Secondly, while some were talking about wearing patches and liked the idea of that scenario playing out in the future, others among us were also thinking along the lines of secrecy and maintaining an inconspicuous presence. I personally appreciated the club patch scenario, but at the same time I was aware that to make money and be off the police radar a crew was much more effective without the major attention-grabbing presence of a gang patch. I was becoming more and more aware of organisations around the world that operated under the strict guidelines of secrecy and although we wouldn't qualify on that level at this stage I did begin to think more along these lines as time went by. For example, there were certain activities that some of us were involved with which simply could not withstand the police scrutiny that comes with the wearing of a gang patch. I knew for a fact that as soon as you put it on you would be ruled out of certain money-making activities. And to top that off I didn't believe the patch was needed. It was unnecessary, people knew who we were, or at least the people that mattered knew who we were.

Around the same time as the drama with Miller was playing out there was another situation developing. Jim was the reasonably well known owner of the Christchurch strip club Calendar Girls. This club was quite popular and there were often a lot of people in there. I had been into Calendar Girls on a number of occasions with the guys. We were friendly with a number of the girls, plus our sergeant-at-arms had some business activities going on with Jim. The sergeant-at-arms was also going out with one of the girls and this lasted for quite a long time. Now, Jim had gotten on the wrong side of a few people around town. One of our members, whom I will refer to as Jethro, met with Jim outside Calendar Girls one night and stabbed him three times in the stomach causing significant damage. According to bystanders he collapsed to the ground and his intestines were falling out onto the footpath. Reports later suggested that he had nearly died. Jethro fled and nearly made it back to his car but the police managed to pick him up along the way. He was arrested and charged with a variety of serious charges.

Over the following months the case was referred to trial and Jethro defended the charges in front of a jury. Jim took the witness stand and identified Jethro as his assailant and testified as to what he saw on that night. He then went on to make claims against our sergeant-at-arms, myself and several others claiming that we were interfering with his strip club and selling drugs in there. As far as I'm aware this was untrue, because I do not recall ever selling any drugs inside Calendar Girls and neither do I recall anyone else selling in there either. The sergeant-at-arms had loaned Jim his cash register and some other property, but I certainly hadn't heard of any interference going on during this period of time. In fact, the sergeant-at-arms was actually in prison leading up to the time that Jim was stabbed, and I did not hear any grumblings from him prior to the stabbing. This ruled him out and also ruled us out because no one else had any financial interest in the club. I think the drug dealing and the interfering was a made-up story, perhaps because Jim didn't want to state the real circumstances surrounding his near-death experience.

Jethro's defence against the charges at the trial was that he had been acting in self-defence against a beer bottle attack. Evidence submitted to the court included photographs of a fresh head wound Jethro had obviously received prior to his arrest, which the defence claimed had happened as a result of the bottle attack. I was called by the defence to discredit the claims of drug dealing and club interference which was successful. One of the girls who worked at the club also denied the claims that we were selling drugs in the club. The defence then went on to paint the picture of Jethro being the innocent victim of an uncalled-for attack and that he had acted out of fear of further injuries. All in all, it was a good defence and one that the jury agreed with. Jethro was acquitted of all the serious charges and only convicted of possession of a knife. This meant that upon sentencing he was immediately released since he had already served his time on remand. I think it would be fair to say that the police were extremely annoyed. Jim would also have been annoyed. What would have been worse for him was the fact that presumably up until then he had considered himself to be something of an underworld player, but now he had taken the stand as a police witness in a police prosecution. What I said in court was a denial of accusations laid against us and the defendant, so I was within my rights to do that because you can defend yourself if charged. For Jim to do what he did virtually disqualified him from any further underworld activity.

Jethro was a free man and was out walking the streets almost immediately upon conclusion of the trial. A lot of people were surprised at how this had played out and there were a lot of rumours circulating around town. One rumour was that Jim had attempted to make a move against us as a crew and that the subsequent near-death experience that followed was a retaliatory hit and a warning to anyone else. They were saying that from the time that Jim had made a move against us to the time that he was hit was less than twelve hours thus giving the impression of speed and strength on the part of those involved in the retaliation. Of course rumours implied that I was the main person responsible and that I should have been in prison for it, but again the courts obviously never came to any of these conclusions.

The song I should have been singing around this time was thank God for His grace and mercy. We were all wicked people void of any morality. This included our crew, Jim, the Boozers and the numerous other people around town who were of the same mentality as us. But many of us were still alive and had chances plus opportunities on the horizon where our unlawful behaviour could be put behind us and our futures transformed. Who would take those opportunities and who would not? That is the question.

The life changing revelation that came to me one night, would for most people probably seem completely ridiculous and maybe even childish. But for me it really was transformative and I have never forgotten this simple lesson ever since the day I saw it. One day we watched a movie called *Braveheart* which is the story about a man that grew up in and around Scotland during the 1200's and then went on to fight for Scotland against the oppressive English armies. If you haven't watched this then it's well worth watching. Let's be clear though, there was a certain amount of the Hollywood brush painted over the story for the purpose of romanticizing the movie and drawing viewers into the plot. This is typical of most movies, where the makers will simplify things by having all the people on one side evil and all the people on the other side good. In the case of *Braveheart* everyone else was evil, except William Wallace and a few of his friends. Life generally isn't really like this, as we all know. In real life the story of William Wallace, Robert the Bruce and the Scottish versus the English was far more complicated and drawn out than what is portrayed in *Braveheart*. Despite this simplification this movie struck a real chord with me. For a start, our family name was Donaldson which comes from the Scottish Clan Donald. Donaldson being a simplification of son of Donald. Likewise, MacDonald, McDonald, MacDonnell and a variety of other modifications are all traced back to the original Clan name Donald and basically mean the same thing, son of Donald. Clan Donald is one of the largest Clans in Scotland. From a young age, I can remember many of my school friends and I were always proud of our Scottish ancestry. Certainly as I was growing up it was something which was important to me. According to history books one of the original chieftains of our Clan, Angus Og MacDonald had taken five thousand of our Clansmen to Bannochburn in support of Robert the Bruce, so this was a fantastic part of history that our Clan could lay claim to. The Scottish Highlanders, in general, no matter what Clan they came from were known for their bravery and hardiness and, most famously, for their courageous defence against a much bigger nation. You can understand why such a movie would have an effect on me. I gained identity from these people and I looked up to them, and this movie was all about them and their way of life.

In this movie the themes of good and evil, righteousness and wickedness, truth and dishonesty were significant. Suddenly I was overwhelmed by a feeling of guilt. It was a magnificent portrayal of the plight of the brave verses the plight of the coward.

The impact this story had on my life is significant to this very day. From that moment forward I began to think about such things. I compared my own ways to that of the characters in the movie and other significant figures who lived a moral life. I realised that I had fallen short and that I needed to change my ways in order to be somebody that I was proud of. Don't get me wrong though, this change did not happen overnight, it was a gradual turn around but from that moment forward it did start to happen. I began to think about the important things, and for the first time in a while, I thought about God again.

The bad news about this was that the beginning point for this recovery was fairly dark; darkness was among us and for some time would continue to be around us. There would be times in the future where it seemed as though life was on the up and then I would be down again and back into the dark. That's just the way it was for a while, but the important thing is that I had had a revelation and on that epiphany building could begin. For now though, I was still in the dark. There were a lot of issues and a lot of travelling before we could even begin to see past the point we were at now.

The fighting continued and our activities were still as bad, if not worse than they had previously been. Right at this stage of my life I found myself around quite a bit of methamphetamine. We called it speed, but it was pure meth mixed with a powder, which would be made into lines and snorted up the nose. The drug was available nearly every day. It was coming from a few senior people who had ties to the original club. This is partly why they trusted me, because they knew I was one of their boys which helped qualify me as a person of trust. I would have bags of speed on me every week and in the space of a week those bags would come and go. It was regular, so I'd be getting topped up every week and I rarely went without. We had some seriously hard times on this stuff, I can certainly assure you of that. We'd be going for weeks and months on it and, man, those times were hard on the body and mind. In a way it was almost a good thing that I was introduced to it at such a young age and suffered as a result, because years later when massive amounts of the pure drug came into Christchurch and flooded the neighbourhoods I had already had previous experience. I knew it was bad and I knew how dangerous it was to take. Years later when other people suffered and literally ruined their lives on meth, I was one of the lucky ones that said no most of the time. Once bitten twice shy you could say. But anyway, that was later on, right now we were into it and going through it like a wildfire, which certainly didn't help our decision-making ability. I guess it was better than being drunk in some circumstances and possibly saved our backsides a few times, but drugs don't make you a better person full stop.

The fights would continue, the incidents would continue, and there were other groups around town that we also had to be aware of such as the Harris gang from Hornby. At this point in time, they were with the Road Knights in Christchurch, and they had a clubhouse on Lincoln Road. One of the fights I had was with one of the Harris brothers who was a Road

Knight member at the time. I got called out to a meeting at the Halswell domain one day where I had a one-on-one with him. A lot of people were surprised that I had fronted up for the fight because the guy I fought had a dangerous reputation and most people were terrified of him. I wasn't too concerned though because I had Uncle with me, and I believed that this guy would be decent enough to settle it the gentleman's way which he did, rather than the situation turning nasty. In fact, that particular Harris brother in the end turned out to be okay contrary to popular belief and I hope he's doing alright because I thought he was a good guy.

Another fight was with a guy from the Sandridge Hotel. My friend and original co-offender, Chris, and his brother had been down at the Sandridge one night by themselves and a few of the locals down there had roughed them up a bit. So they came and told us, and we immediately jumped into our cars and took off down there. We filed into the pub and there would have been a line of about fifteen of us, but when we got inside none of the culprits were there. The locals were counting us as we came in and it didn't hurt to have a bit of a show of force like that to remind them not to muck around. Even though the main ones weren't there, word definitely would have got back to them. I knew who one of them was so after a week or two had gone by, I managed to find him down there drinking again in the middle of the day, I shot inside and wrenched him down to the ground by grabbing a couple of handfuls of hair on either side of his head. I gave him a good telling off in front of everyone. There would have been fifty odd people standing in the bar watching me swing this guy around. He was probably fifteen years older than me and a good twenty kilograms heavier. Nobody said a word, apart from this woman over the back who started yelling at me to leave him alone. But it wasn't that bad, I was just giving him a bit of a wind up to get him back. Those guys were fine with me after that incident.

Funnily enough I found that guy from prison with the skinheads tattooed on the back of his head in the Sandridge Hotel as well. He was playing poker machines in the gaming room when I walked in there one day. I recognised him and his tattoo straight away and let loose at him with a not too over the top telling off. I did not hurt him though, because I guess I felt a bit sorry for him. Definitely didn't look as big as he did last time, and he appeared to acknowledge that he had done wrong when I hit him up about it. I said to him that he was lucky I was starting to change my ways otherwise I could have easily pulled him to pieces. He acknowledged that and said he knew who I was now. Satisfied that I had made my point, I turned my back and walked out.

Then there was the time I took on eight Back Yard Boozers in a car by myself in the middle of Moorhouse Ave. The story goes like this. I had spent the night with this beautiful woman by the name of Kresta. We were returning from Diamond Harbour and the plan was for me to drop her off on the way into town. We had just had some lines a half an hour before and so both of us were feeling energised as I dropped her off at the prearranged address. I left her there, pulled out onto Moorhouse Ave and within a few minutes I realised that there was a large American style yank tank traveling alongside me. I looked at the occupants and realised the car was full of guys with bald heads and tattoos; perhaps as many as eight guys in there because as I said it was a big wagon and they seemed to be packed in it to the max. Then I looked again and realised that I recognised two of them. Two of them were Boozers, that I was sure of. And as far as I was concerned if two of them were Boozers then all of them were. A rush of thoughts came through my mind all at once. It was true that I had been anxious about running into a pack of these guys in a difficult situation. Its only common sense that if you are in the wrong place at the wrong time and you run into guys like that when you're not prepared then it could definitely get messy.

So, I had thought about this previously and I concluded that I should give it to them as hard as I possibly could if that situation arose. As I've previously mentioned there has to be a deterrent and there is the psychological deterrent whereby you show absolutely no fear towards them. The best option was to take them on in a not so dangerous place like this rather than mistakenly running into them in a not so favourable situation where the odds might be against me. After all, how much damage could they really get away with in the middle of a busy Christchurch street? I didn't think they'd have much time to do anything. With that in mind I pulled up right beside them until I made eye contact and then I gave them the fingers and abused them through the window.

I continued to abuse them for about one hundred metres as we drove side by side down the middle of Moorhouse. Things were going according to plan until the lights went red in front of me and I was forced to slow down and come to a halt. It was right on the corner of Moorhouse, and Fitzgerald Ave and they had a free turn, but much to my disappointment their car also came to a stop in the middle of the free turn. Luckily for them it wasn't that busy which gave two of them time to jump out while the car and the rest of them sidled around the corner and waited. I watched as two of them approached my car which was still waiting at the lights and in a split second, I made the decision to do it. I was going to defend. I flung the car door open and bounced around to the other side of the car to confront them. I was lucky more of them hadn't piled out of the car to come across and fortunate again that neither of the two that had approached appeared to be overly intimidating. In fact, I knew one of them. I had realised it straight away but both of us were in the moment and the fact was that neither of us could back down by this stage. The one I knew was one of the extras we had taken along with us to do the hit on Paul Sutherland. Since that time, a few years earlier when we had been to jail together, he had joined up with the

Boozers and was now one of their members. There was not much I could do, even though I knew him I was still his enemy and any chance he would have had to take me down he would have done it, so I had to carry on and put anything like that behind me. The second guy that I didn't know had now moved over towards my car with a knuckle duster and it appeared as if he was trying to make a distraction by hitting my car which would then give the first guy the chance to have a go at me. But it didn't work because the first guy wasn't making a move which allowed me to advance on the guy with the knuckle duster. The reports say I got him right between the eyes with a wheel brace and a stream of blood flowed down his face within a split second of the impact. With rows of cars now parked up behind us and bystanders looking on, the two Boozers decided a retreat was in order and took off back to the waiting car. People were looking at me trying to work out what was going on, so I jumped straight back in the car and drove off in the direction of my friend's house. I never heard a single word about the incident from police. I guess anyone who was watching saw that it was two verses one and assumed I was acting in self-defence.

That wasn't the end of it though as later that evening after I had stopped in at Kresta's house for a couple of hours we got the report inside that my car was on fire out on the street. We went out and had a look and sure enough the car had been firebombed and was totally gutted. Luckily it was not an overly expensive car.

CHAPTER 12

DARKNESS III

There weren't too many more incidents like that involving Boozers to report. I think there were a couple of house visits that went on including when Rick caught Shane Hobbs in the driveway of his house and hit him on the nose, but generally speaking things quietened down after a while and eventually the Boozers closed down altogether. Some of them went off and did other things, some joined different groups and really, they were never heard from again after that except as individuals. I actually ran into a few of them over the years but after ten years or more had past a lot of people are not interested anymore regardless of what happened. Those guys were alright, I guess. Just young and hey what else can you say? Let them be.

For us as a group there were greater challenges on the horizon. Money was one of those challenges and that is what would soon be on a lot of peoples minds rather than fighting. Money and progress. To get to that point though, I personally had another bridge to cross.

That bridge would be another short stint in prison. Basically, we had kept on living the same life without giving it a second thought and we'd done it for too long. Firstly, we were blamed for swiping another strip club owner over in town. That was Terry Brown. Terry Brown was labelled by the media as the godfather of the Christchurch Sex Industry. Yes, he was a bit of a bad dude and he'd once been a patch member of a club in town, but I don't think he was quite as much of a big deal as the media always made him out to be. I certainly know a lot of people didn't like him and especially a number of the old club didn't like him. Terry had been beaten up a couple of times by members of the original club and also one time he was stabbed at the club house. According to the older fellas he was getting smart to one of the members one day and that member ended up stabbing him and throwing him out the gate. So, he definitely wasn't liked by our older guys. In particular the sergeant-at-arms hated Terry.

The sergeant-at-arms was in prison again by this stage and on the night in question myself and a large contingent of our guys had gone into the Dolls House Strip Club which Terry owned. That same night Terry was knocked out twice in his own Strip Club whilst his security were trying to separate him and protect him. He was then pushed down a full flight of stairs after his security lost track of him and then he was attacked again at the bottom and kicked in the head multiple times. According to reports he had been carried off down the street by his security with his head beaten up like a basketball and the fall down the stairs was lucky not to have killed him. The rumours started to circulate again and obviously people thought it was us because we were the ones who were in there. They also said I was the one who had knocked out Terry twice and thrown him down the stairs, but they stopped short of suggesting that I'd attacked him at the bottom of the stairs. I won't comment much further other than to say that I never heard anything about police involvement or investigations.

The incident that cost me six months in jail was probably the one incident I should have been found not guilty on. I still believe that if I had stood up in court and told the story as it happened and defended those charges then I would have been found not guilty. Instead my friend told me to leave it to the lawyer and then when the lawyer made the same suggestion, I just kept my mouth shut and let him do the talking. I'm sure they would have believed me if I'd had the chance because it's just so easy to sound honest when you are telling the truth.

In any case what happened is that I was visiting a friend of mine in Hornby on the night that this unravelled. This was a friend of a few years and I had previously had quite a bit to do with him. He was a Māori fella, quite a good sort and had been a supporter of the Handlebars club for a reasonable amount of time. It was through this friend that I met the older guys of the Handlebars club and between the two of us we had done a bit of wheeling and dealing together over the years. I was just parked up there having a cup of tea and a bit of a catch up, when another guy that I had met before came around and told us this big story about how he had been picking up his children from these people's house and one of them had punched him in the head. So, this guy was really my friend's friend, but I did know him from meeting him around there. The guy was not a bad sort and my friend trusted him, so we requested more information about what had happened. According to him these people had been looking after his children and when he went there to pick them up, he found all these people sitting around drinking beer and acting like slobs. So, he said something to one of them who had subsequently jumped up and punched him in the head. Now he wanted someone to go with him to the house so he could have a one-on-one with the guy. He needed support because he thought there were heaps of them there. It didn't sound too bad to us, so the three of us and another fella that happened to show up at the same time all jumped in the cars and headed around there. We first dropped the vehicles off at the guy's house who we were helping and then walked the few hundred metres around the corner from there. We got there and all of us stood out the front reasonably respectfully and just kept our mouths shut while the guy we were helping called his opponent out for a one-on-one. The guy came out and they had a one-on-one on the lawn which appeared to be fairly mild if you ask me and our guy won, so we assumed it would all be over now and turned to slowly move off. This is where I started to think this guy we were helping was a bit of a weird one because he just started jogging off down the road and left the three of us by ourselves. Suddenly a large mob of young adults swarmed out onto the road from within the property and moved towards us in an aggressive manner.

This is where it gets confusing, because we had just witnessed a fair one-on-one fight where nobody was seriously hurt and now this entire party wanted to carry it on. And that is what they did, they literally came up to us and tried to attack us. We were outnumbered five to one and the only advantage we had over them was that we were carrying a couple of heavy cricket wickets each and the other guy had a cricket bat. So here we were, three verses about fifteen or twenty and it turned nasty really fast. They were coming at us from all directions, and we just had to swat them off one after the other. I broke both wickets in the space of about five minutes until all I had left was about three inches poking out either side of my hands. Even then I was about to start using it as a poker but at the last second my Māori friend came over and pulled me out from in the middle of it and said, "Let's go". By this time our opponents were bloodied and beaten but still half heartedly following us up the street. All this time the guy that we were supposed to be helping was no-where to be seen. He had left from the outset.

You can probably understand now why I believed we were innocent because we had only been there to stop this other guy getting mobbed. When we tried to leave peacefully afterwards we got attacked ourselves. Cops turned up at the guy's house where our cars were, arrested us and that's basically the end of the story. All the guys from the party wrote statements against us and appeared in court testifying against us. That was that.

Maybe this would not be such a bad thing after all if you consider the bigger picture. A year ago, I had been living at the old club president's house and attempting to make a way forward. He and his wife had been kind enough to put me up for a while until I was able to get a few loose ends tidied up and sort myself out a bit. It was nearing the end of a fairly lengthy run of partying and shady business, so I was really grateful for somewhere quiet to park up. After a while, I was given the opportunity by another friend in town to come on board with something a little bit risky. It was worth money though, so I had agreed to go along with it. So, I left the president's house and moved into central Christchurch where I began this little operation. The longer I was involved with this operation the more uncomfortable I had become with it. It just didn't feel right, and the reality is that I was still in the middle of Christchurch, still lining myself up for trouble and it is possible that it could have turned ugly if the afore mentioned incident hadn't happened instead. I guess what I'm trying to say is that perhaps the fight outside the party and the short-term prison sentence might have actually been a better result than the first option of staying in town and carrying on with what I was doing.

What ended up happening was I was bailed to my friend Baker's house in Temuka. The courts stipulated that I wasn't allowed North of the Rakaia River as a part of my bail conditions. I stayed with Baker for some time, and we still managed to get up to a bit of misbehaviour even way down there where it was nice and quiet. Overall it was a peaceful stay. Then for the first time in what seemed like a considerable amount of time I got a job working on a deer farm in Sheffield and stayed there for the best part of a year while I waited for the court process to unfold. That was a great time on the farm during that period and funnily enough I made some good connections which in the years to come would be greatly beneficial to me.

After the trial and the surprise of the conviction I ended up back out at Paparoa Prison doing another six months. Prior to the prison sentence, a lot eventuated in the space of a few short years and it wasn't all fighting. There was money, jealousy, betrayal, drugs, politics and even murders that took place around us. All these ingredients culminated to send me in the direction that I would eventually take.

Five scuffles happened in between the Terry Brown incident and the eventual sentencing for my last and final incarceration. Firstly, on a separate night to the one I previously mentioned regarding Terry Brown, we were up at the Dolls House again. I had a run in with two of Jim's guys when they tried to follow me into the toilet with a bottle. It was a completely failed attempt as I simply pushed them out of my way and walked straight out the toilet door. For a couple of big guys, they were pretty useless. And to think one of them was Jim's famed big shot Tuala. Following this incident, or around the same time, our crew seemed to be going through some pressures as all circles do and I felt that I had been treated a little unfairly by a few of the guys. This resulted in a minor incident with one of my friends and a slightly heavier one with another of our friends where I gave him a few punches in the head. Possibly even for our level of justice it may not have been the right thing to do but I did it nonetheless. On another occasion out at the Hororata Hog Out one of the ex-Handlebar members took a swing at me as several of us including the sergeant-at-arms and a couple of them stood around together. This ex-Handlebar member was drunk, and I don't even know if he knew what he was doing, but it was a completely failed attempt as I just shifted my head a few inches backwards and watched it swing past me in an almost slow-motion event. I was about to grab a hold of him but our sergeant-at-arms calmed it down straight

GANGLAND TO GUINEA

away. It is a little bit humorous I guess when you think about it now. The Handlebars member knew me through the sergeant-at-arms and a few bike transactions in town but there was nothing really in it, I don't think. I and the sergeant-at-arms had a brawl together at the Darfield pub too which I shouldn't leave out. Not him versus me but us versus a few locals. Nothing serious.

Moving on to the prison incidents, I found a Hammer skin gang member in the cells at the Christchurch district courts who had somehow wronged me in the past, so I chased him around the holding cell trying to get my hands on him but to no avail because he kept using the fixed concrete table as a barrier in between us. What's more, one of the Asian guys in the cell with us went to stick up for him for some reason and so I had a near scuffle with the Asian guy as well. The Asian guy was a big, well-known guy too and just as we got started one of the court guards witnessed what we were doing and went to put charges on them because he thought that they were causing the problem. This Asian guy got a big fright when I yelled at the guard to stay out of it, and the guard then obeyed what I had said. Straight away the Asian guy wanted to be my friend after that.

The second time I went to prison was a lot quieter and I spent most of my time out at the drug unit in Rolleston which was very peaceful. I completed several NZQA qualifications and spent the rest of the time in the gym pumping weights and boxing with two other trained boxers. It was actually a great time because I would have been training for at least a few hours a day five days a week. The only disruption I faced out there was from a couple of guys who were a few years my senior and probably weighed ten kilograms more than I did. A Māori and a white guy that thought they were the men in the drug unit. Yes, definitely a few guys feared them, but I didn't, so when they tried to short-change me on some tobacco I came back at them straight away. I ended up stepping them both out together in front of about thirty people and we agreed on a time to meet at the gym the next day where we would fight it out. Most people thought it was pretty funny, but the two guys didn't and within a few hours they came back to me with a second pottle of tobacco to make up the difference plus an offer to put it behind us which we agreed upon. I did meet some good guys in there on that occasion including my first meeting with the ex-president of the Road Knights. He was a good guy too and he was housed right next to me for three months before I was let out. The only other funny incident that occurred while I was in Rolleston was that Jim phoned an ex-Knight in there and paid him NZ$500 to attack me. Jim had no idea that I was good friends with this ex-Road Knight fella and so paid the money without even thinking about it. My friend took the money and immediately had half of it transferred into my prison account so the pair of us sat there for the next two weeks chowing down on goodies from Jim's money. That wouldn't be the last Jim heard from me though as a reasonable amount of time later on, I bailed Jim up outside his strip club, challenging him to a one on one fight. He didn't want to tempt fate this last time and walked straight into his strip club and out of harms way.

I left Rolleston Prison this time feeling pretty positive and determined not to come back. While in there I had realised that things had to change for me. I'd previously had the revelation about good verses evil which I really meant to incorporate into my way of life and now I was beginning to realise that I simply had to have more direction in my life. I had to have goals, dreams and follow through. No longer could we be fighting for the scraps at the bottom, we needed to be living a life of accomplished dreams and happiness because otherwise what's the point.

I moved into a spare room at Uncle's ex-girlfriend Shell's house and got set up as best as I could. Soon after I was working full time and on track for some big changes. When I think back on that first year after my release I kind of wonder what I was actually doing because an entire year just went by like that, so fast. From memory I think it was a fairly quiet time. A lot of the guys were settling down and trying to stay out of trouble. Obviously, there were various activities going on but not anything major that springs to mind. Things also quietened down with our club activities. We were no longer pushing to buy a property, and the talk about putting on a patch had all but disappeared. A lot of the guys were thinking about money and staying out of the limelight. Of course, most of us retained that club connection and loyalty to one another but overall, I believe most of us were taking time out to reflect. My personal ambition was to gain a qualification and set up a way forward which didn't necessarily involve breaking the law. I and a few of the others still saw ourselves as a crew but, rather than a commitment to any major criminal gang, it was more of a commitment to each other and backing each other up. A lot of the guys never stopped breaking the law that's a fact, but I think everyone calmed down a bit and took a step back. I moved a few times over the next year or so and kept working on and off. Admittedly even though my ambition was for legitimacy, I did carry on with a few activities that brought in a bit of extra cash on the side. This meant I could still have my luxury items like the motorbikes and the ability to enjoy life. I was still planning though; I was on a mission to get educated but it was just a matter of timing and getting everything in order so that could happen.

I'm trying to recall if at this stage I had been thinking anymore about the spiritual realm and God, but I do believe that this was still a year or two off. The push for now was to just keep going forward and be prepared for my first year at university. Quite a few small events occurred leading up to my time at university and even a small event can create ripples, so it is definitely worth mentioning these events. First, my friend Chris did something quite weird one night and came onto Uncle's girlfriend. It seems crazy to me because I cannot for the life of me work out why he would want to do that, but he did do it and so shortly afterwards Chris splintered away from the group. Uncle wanted to take him out big time but instead he was pushed away, and we never really had anything to do with him again. I have spoken to Chris in recent years and it sounds like he is doing okay, but the hard truth of it is that he has spent over fifty percent of his life in jail. First, he stabbed someone half to death in Hornby totally unrelated to us and then he did it again a few years later. So, most of the time I've been out he's been locked up. The next person to lose the plot was Baker. He was over at Jethro's one night visiting and there was some cosiness going on between him and Jethro's girlfriend after Jethro had gone to sleep early. Nothing happened as far as I am aware, but it was enough to upset Jethro significantly and subsequently blew a big hole in our crew for a second time because Jethro wanted Baker out. Not long after that Baker packed up and moved north. Again, he was still there, and people talked to him off and on, but he was no longer one of us. He was out.

The sergeant-at-arms by this stage was attempting to lay low after he had been involved in another high-profile murder case a few years earlier. He was never charged but we were unlucky enough to know some of the people that police accused. In fact, they were looking at the sergeant-at-arms too but in the end, they only charged one person. So, the sergeant-at-arms was now living well out in the rural areas and trying to lead a healthy, sensible life. Next person to cause a ripple was Uncle. Uncle found himself over at the Christchurch Road Knights clubhouse and before we knew it, he had decided he wanted to prospect. So, he started prospecting for them and really in the space of only a short period of time we were down several guys, and our activities were down to nearly zero as well. Everyone was off doing their own thing. So, I guess this was the perfect time for me, I was off to Lincoln University the following year and almost all the activities and avenues for distraction were shut down. At least for now they were.

I started at Lincoln University in 2005. I was twenty-six and with a fair bit of life experience behind me I thought I could make a good go of things. As it happened, I did make a good go of it and in the first year I passed seven out of eight papers. A degree was made up of twenty-four papers so having passed seven in my first year meant that I had basically completed a third of the degree. I was happy and set up for the second year, but as that second year approached things began to derail. Uncle had left the Road Knights by this stage and had moved back into town, so effectively we had him back with us. At the same time there was a major influx of methamphetamine into Christchurch. Ice they called it; this was the rock version. Pure and extremely addictive. Heaps of the guys were getting into it and nearly all my friends were either on it or involved with it. Uncle told me to come over one day and visit him in town which I did. It was one of those moments where you just knew you should not be going, but I never listened to that inner voice. Instead, I went over and visited him and there was another old friend there who I had not seen for ages and things took a downward spiral from there.

They say everything happens for a reason and I believe it. I am happy now and what happened back then only strengthened me for the future. God probably knew the day I was born that I was going to go through it, and I think he just made plans for me to work around those times.

Funnily enough before this next dark period of my life started, I had actually been reading a book on positive thinking. You could laugh about that and say it kicked into action a few years too late but nevertheless at least it kicked in at the end. Believe it or not I had even walked into a church during that year at university too. I remember walking down the road praying. I kept praying the same prayers over and over hoping that something would happen and, it would happen eventually, but not when I wanted it to. They say these things take time.

The financial toll of the way I had lived my life up until now was starting to build up. I now had some bad debt. I had court fines sitting there unpaid. I owed my mother money too, which I really hated because I never wanted to be the type of person that would end up owing his mother money. The courts were giving me grief about the unpaid fines and reparation, then I had to switch cars again after they impounded one of them. I had already sold my Ducati, the Motor Guzzi and then the BMW before I had even got to university. Before the second year rolled around I had almost ground to a complete halt. Yes, it is true that I could have ground my way out of it and perhaps not partied with the guys over the summer break and maybe I could have gone on from there to be a success, but it didn't happen. I knew a way that I could make a lot of money in a hurry, and I just gave in. I guess if I had a moment in my life that I know I should feel guilty about, that was it. That was it. But I am not going to live a life of self-condemnation. I am going to move on and never make that mistake again!

CHAPTER 13

THE LAST YEARS BEFORE THE LIGHT

Very soon I was living back in Christchurch. I stayed with Uncle for a while, and we had some good times together again. I was catching up with Jethro quite a bit, and a few of the other guys as well. There were a second lot of young guys coming through who were like our younger brothers. There was a bit of potential among them. Also, there was a beautiful woman I had noticed and to be honest I put a bit of time into chasing her, but nothing really came of it. I wasn't in the right place, and she was probably definitely not the right woman for me. One of our good friends lived in town and so I was catching up with him regularly. This big fella had actually been around right from the beginning. Even in the early days right back at the beginning when I was fourteen at the club he was there. He had never been a member of the original club. Instead, he had been a member of a different motorcycle club which had folded, so when we started our new club up in Waterloo Road, he came over and immediately joined with us. He had been there the entire time through everything I have talked about. He was a good sort; he was intelligent and one of those people that others tend to like. He has always been my good friend and he probably will be in the future as well.

Anyway, the sergeant-at-arms was floating in and out of town a little. I still regularly saw the old president and whenever I got a chance, I would still go out of my way to catch up with the older original patch members. I always thought it was important to keep connected with them as much as possible. I guess they were family in a way. But as nice as it was to keep connected with those we cared about, I also had business to take care of. I had money to get on top of, courts to deal with and a lot of stuff to get sorted. Another thing that is worth mentioning is that even though I was back in town again and mixing with the old crew again, something had started to change within me. I mean, I know it sounds silly that I was about to get involved in criminal activity again, but at the same time I was thinking about doing the right thing. I was even praying and thinking about possibly going to church at some stage. Heck, the reality is that I was still a mixed-up guy but there was hope. There was a small flame starting to burn, it was really, really small and possibly you could say it was just smouldering, but something was changing.

Within a short period of time, I had moved into my own apartment in town. However, the operation I was about to get involved with started off slowly. After a few months I asked my friend what his problem was and why were we not getting stuck into the project as we had planned, and he straight out told me that he was paranoid and that he had enough on his plate already. Then he suggested I take over and he was happy to give me his half of everything which he did. So, I was out on my own and from then on things took off fast. I was doing a lot of stuff and pretty soon I went from financial difficulty to financially okay. From that perspective everything was looking really good. And I had time on my hands as well, I could pick and choose what I wanted to do with my time. I had a bit of work on here and there and even kept working for the same farmer I had been working for when I was at university. He was a good guy to work for and I enjoyed being out in the country getting my hands dirty and keeping healthy. But it was not all rosy times ahead of course. There were some big challenges that would be coming my way soon and it really was by the grace of God that I made it through without too many hassles.

My intentions were not necessarily bad, but because of the way we lived our lives we were easily drawn into bad practice. When over half of the people you deal with daily are criminally minded, gang members or drug users, again it's easy to become corrupted. There is the theory that once you have been out for long enough and have fully transformed your own life then you can go back and help others with their lives. But this was not the case for me. I had barely been away for a year and now I was straight back amongst them attempting to do two things at the same time. It is like I was drawn between two worlds. In one instance I wanted to pay off my bills, go back to study and spend some time in church, and at the same time here I was having thoughts about how I could maximise my profit, maintain a crew based around defence and a lot more. That is why I said I was mixed up because it was like there were two different sides to me. One worry was that I still had this persistent almost gravitational pull towards the idea of running a defence crew. I was not interested in running a criminal syndicate or organisation, so it was not a criminal gang desire but rather the desire for our own underworld crew based on defence. So, still bad because it led to more violence but not as bad as the desire for criminality. The other drawback that I had was the involvement in money making outside the bounds of normally accepted methods. When you have one foot in the dark side its very hard to pull that foot back out again no matter how innocent your intentions may be. The fact is I had even created a justification for the money making that I was involved with. In my mind

I had declared this activity as a service to the rebellious section of society. As in, when people refuse to go elsewhere for help then they can come to me and therefore my service is not necessarily evil. This kind of thinking is what I like to call mental gymnastics. Unfortunately, it is used throughout the world we live in every day, and it basically acts as a way of saying, "my evil is justified because of this reason". That is how it works but the reality that people really need to understand is that this is not truth.

The self-help book I read a couple of years before had stated that if what you are doing with your life does not match up with your personal values then you can never be successful. Therefore, if you know something to be wrong but continue to do it you are almost definitely setting yourself up to fail. I agree with this notion and even if you do not quite go so far as outright failure the side effects of what you know to be wrong are at the very least going to cause you some problems. This is exactly what happened with my situation. I did not fail as such, but I had some very real challenges that I had to deal with along the way. Of my two main areas of concern, the first and most prevalent was the desire for the defence crew which lead to an abundance of violence. I tallied up thirty-seven fights in my first count, then I have referenced roughly another sixteen incidents since then and moving on from there it wouldn't improve straight away. Even though I had this new vision of righteousness and honour I was still resolving issues with violence.

On another occasion there had been a Nissan Cefiro stolen from one of our young guy's addresses in Waltham. He was adamant that it had been a large Black Power associate from a few blocks away who had stolen the car, so ten of us went around to the house and under my own strength I ripped his security door off the side of his house. It was one of those strong mesh screen ones. I still do not know how I did it because it was basically welded in place. While I was doing this the Black Power guy let his dog out through the gap to attack me, but as soon as the dog caught the edge of my boot it went straight back in the house. This was a surprise because it was not any small lap dog. All the young guys were spinning out because they had never seen anyone deal with a situation like that before. The Black Power guy was freaking too. Another time I broke a guy's nose at the Irish bar Micky Finns in town, splattering blood over the woman he had just insulted.

Then there were a couple of problems in Addington. My friend who had a house off Selwyn Street had two separate guys renting a room at his house at different times. The first one was a meth dealer. The meth dealer had swindled our female friend out of a few thousand dollars, so I bailed the guy up in the back yard and knocked his front teeth out. A while later the second renter moved in, and we later found out by his own admission that his daughter gave an affidavit against him stating that he had molested her. I really did not like that guy anyway because he had been shooting up morphine in my friend's house and then encouraging him to do it as well. As soon as we saw the typed affidavit against this guy, we literally threw him out of the house by the scruff of his neck. Another time I was doing community work over at Orton Bradley Park to pay off my fines and reparation, when a guy who did not like me called me a nark behind my back and one of the other guys told me about it. The story goes that one of the other workers distracted the boss man by asking him for a ride to the toilet block and while they were gone the guy who had called me a nark was attacked. Apparently, he was beaten around the lunchroom until he had a broken nose. There was quite a bit of blood on the concrete floor afterwards which was swiftly washed away with buckets of water before the boss man came back. When I finally finished doing all my community work months later, the boss man, who I ended up getting along with quite well, told me that he thought it was me who had beaten the guy up, but I never commented on the situation with him.

Unfortunately, there were a couple of times the young guys got a bit of a hurry up. My friend Neil got a few punches in the head as a warning one day after he had wound me up. Then another young guy who we are still good friends with had twenty thousand dollars' worth of stuff stolen out of his garage that belonged to us. He received a bit of a hiding for that too but it was not me that time. I knocked another one over at our friend's house just around the corner from there after they became drunk and out of control at a party one night. So, like I said there was just little incidents going on all the time. This mad couple tried to attack me on Brougham Street one day in the middle of their road rage incident, so I knocked the guy right on his jaw to wake him up.

Then there was the Chinese guy at Subway. My friend had just had an operation on his stomach and you could still see the stitches, but this Chinese guy would not leave him alone, so I knocked him about three times in the head while I was still holding my filled roll in the other hand. Another time we had a false alarm at Uncle's place. We turned up there with machetes and bats and we were about to lop some guy's arm off until we discovered that the perpetrators were gone. This one demonstrates how quickly situations could escalate when we believed we were an authority unto ourselves.

Another time I was sitting at home one day just relaxing and all the young guys turned up at my house in a Bedford van. They wanted me to come with them and help them out at this big brawl at a park in Brighton. So, I said, "Yeah, no worries", and jumped in the van with them. We turned up at this park and there were about one hundred of us all on the same side. I had never seen anything like this before, I mean I did not even know most of these guys. I thought it was simply crazy and even on the way out there

I was having to calm some of them down and talk some sense into them because they wanted to kill somebody. I told them in no uncertain terms that we were not killing anyone today. Thankfully, they listened to me. Finally, when the poor opposition team of about twenty stragglers came winding their way through the trees towards us and saw us all lined up there like a mob of football hooligans they all immediately turned around and started jogging their way back in the same direction they had just come. All our guys let out this roar as if we were in the middle of a *Braveheart* movie and the entire mob of young fellas chased these guys down through the trees and out onto a street on the other side of the park. The opposition were lucky to have made it to the street where they probably felt at least a little bit safer, because if the guys had caught them in the trees, it could have gotten ugly. Our guys poured out onto the street and surrounded this little group. On the street, we older guys did our best to maintain a really relaxed attitude and do what ever we could to make sure these guys walked away without any injuries. As it turned out they completely denied any knowledge of the prearranged fight and said that we "had the wrong guys". Of course, they were lying, but I don't think anyone really cared now that we had them on the back foot. It was just a show of force and once everyone was satisfied that that had been achieved the young guys were happy to let them go. Just another day in paradise for us.

In-between the fighting during those years, I did try to keep busy. I had a fair bit on which included part time work, training at the gym, boxing, paying off my reparations and fines through community work, and of course the other activities I was doing on the side. Then there were the hobbies which included hunting, the motorbikes, reading and a lot more. Unfortunately, around this time the methamphetamine had worked its way through our circles and a lot of people were doing it. Thankfully, I had already been through my own personal meth problem a number of years earlier, so I was already experienced and was able to avoid such problems again. I did get into it to a certain degree, just not to the same level as everyone else. I also had come to a personal conviction that meth dealing was quite evil and corrupt. Previously when we had at times been involved with larger amounts of meth, I had experienced this overwhelming feeling of being a terrible person. Soon I realised that this feeling was exactly what it was. We have all heard the saying "It is what it is", and this expression is normally used in a different way than the way I am using it, but I think that the way I am now using it is correct for this notion. It is, what it is. If you can feel that feeling, then it is probably your conscious or subconscious trying to tell you something. I must give credit to a great family doctor we had over the years who I am extremely grateful to for all the assistance and support he has given us. This doctor was a Christian doctor, and my mother was friends with his wife. One time when I was in my early twenties, I went to see him, and I told him that I was feeling depressed and unhappy. His response was perfect, and I have remembered it. He looked at me and he said, "That's probably because you are not doing much with your life". Absolutely correct and that again was another turning point in my life, not because he showed me sympathy but because he told the truth. This also ties in with what I am saying, you feel bad because you are doing bad.

So as I said, I had already experienced the meth problem previously and I had experienced what I would call revelations about certain things which would help prevent me getting involved at the same level that others were involved. Most importantly I would never be involved with the dealing or manufacture of meth from that time forward. The guys and I still liked to party and socialise together though, and we ended up doing a lot of it around this time probably because the quality of the drugs was so good at that point in time. We would party for weeks on end and what made it worse was that we had money. Most of us had money and for us we could easily smoke one thousand dollars worth of meth in one night. Easily without even thinking about it. The reality is that this turned into a bit of a hectic time for a while there, and there was soon to be consequences suffered. Yes, I had a fairly stable way of life with the work and the training and other activities going on, but these extended periods of partying became more and more frequent, and things started to happen. I guess what helped me out through this period was that I was one of the smart ones who knew when you had to stop. Other people around town were going hard and taking meth as if it were marijuana which caused them massive problems. My approach was if you can't help yourself from doing it then just do it once a month. Do not do it every week and especially not every day. Other people did not realise this and totally destroyed their lives. I have heard of guys dying from heart attacks, people spending years in mental asylums, people walking around totally malnourished and messed up with missing teeth and the like. Basically, half of New Zealand's underworld became junkies in the space of a year. This destroyed what used to be a semi-blue-collar, middle-class group of people. This is another example of God's grace which kept me from being a number like the rest of them.

I do believe that what did happen to me during this time though was a combination of things. Firstly, we were doing too much partying, so all of us started to get a little bit out of control. I could feel animosity building amongst us. For example, I did not feel as if I could trust the sergeant-at-arms or Uncle anymore. I believed there was talk or mutterings going on among the group that I thought amounted to betrayal. It is often hard to pinpoint that kind of thing, but I do believe things were changing. For a while there I also became a little unwell. The drugs were affecting me and the stress of having to perform and get through this difficult stage of my life created a dangerous mixture. The unwellness threw me off track and was a bit of a shock, but at the same time I believe it was a blessing in disguise because I reduced the amount of partying and bad behaviour right down to a much lower level. I basically stopped all drug use and focused seriously on health again.

Another factor that needs to be mentioned is that during those last few years I started to look around me at the people I had lived my life with, and I realised that I did not want to end up like them. A lot of the guys had broken marriages, children all over the place, some were in jail and very few of the guys had what I would have considered to be a happy life. A lot of the woman who were in the scene were also just as crazy and messed up as us, which made me think, "How I can possibly start to get on track with an environment like this?" Even if I found a woman that I liked living this life, there is no way I could ever truly trust her. But it was as if the other guys were oblivious to these obvious facts. Even if I tried to talk to some of the guys and discuss some of these issues they could not see what I was talking about. In fact, I think some of these conversations may have even put some of the guys on edge around me and possibly this is where some of the animosity towards me was coming from. I had been to church a few times by this stage as I went about trying to work through some of the issues I was facing and because I wanted to be around some different people. Perhaps I would gain some additional strength through this process I thought. But it felt like the more steps I took in one direction to better myself, aggravations would spring up at the other end of my social network. I guess I am suggesting that these occurrences were not coincidences but rather a result of how others view someone who starts to make changes that are not in line with their normal behaviour.

Jethro and I came to blows one day as we were discussing the possibility of a more structured approach to our crew. It was a fight; we were punching each other in the head. It was a silly disagreement though, because the point that we got hung up on was not necessarily that important. But it was the way that Jethro reacted that immediately made me realise that Uncle had been attempting to undermine me. I knew straight away that these guys had been discussing things when I was not in the room. I had sensed that Uncle was like that for a long time, and I knew the sergeant-at-arms was definitely like that, because I had heard him rubbishing even ex-members of the original club. One day I told him I did not want to hear it because he was doing it in front of a woman and that day was a turning point too. I realised that Uncle and the sergeant-at-arms were starting to go funny on it. They had both had too many drugs and the lives that they had lived were starting to mess with them. I could tell this was not good and our relationships started to erode from that point on. How could you trust guys that would mouth off about their own members in front of outsiders? That is the exact reason that Miller got punished, because he was doing it. Could these guys not understand that strength comes from unity and secrecy. People fear what they do not know or understand. When these guys started 'opening up' and talking about each other and everyone in the circle like it was nothing, it totally undermined the entire effort of everything we had ever done together. I just could not understand how they could ignore this.

There was another reality that we had to face now which became plainly obvious to me and that was that this environment we were living in was so unbelievably negative. Uncle and others would sit around and talk about others and nearly everything that came out of their mouths was just negative. I can remember Uncle talking and he would just put crap on everyone. Individuals were rubbished, other crews and clubs were rubbished, straight people were rubbished, even old-school, hard men who had lived their life in the most honourable way that an old biker could were still not safe. All it took was one mistake and that person was written off for ever. Lifelong friends were written off as nothing but scum. I realised that if these guys were not safe then what made me think that I was safe? Was it only through the threat of severe violence that people are safe in this world? Or if they maintain a blind loyalty to a failing system? Well, I did not want to have a blind loyalty to a failing system and nor could I maintain a threat of severe violence forever. At some stage I am going to get old or sick and then my ability to maintain that threat would be diminished.

I realised Uncle was working against me when I spoke to Uncle after the fight with Jethro. Uncle immediately gave it away. Now I knew and things changed. Who knows exactly why they went against me, maybe it was jealousy, maybe because I was talking out of line when we were discussing topics like right living, maybe they knew about the church meetings which I'd been keeping a secret, but whatever it was they didn't have my back like they used to. Yes, officially we were still brothers in the life, but really my faith in their ability to look out for me was gone. It was history. I knew straight away that this life of ours was over. How did I know that? One very simple answer to a simple question gave me all the information that I needed to say we were done. The question was, if some opposition person killed me or put me in a wheelchair, who out of these guys would retaliate and do something about it? I realised that nobody would have done anything. Years ago, they would have, but now they wouldn't. That's how I knew it was over. I realised I was the only one left who was fighting.

There was still the possibility that I would be hit and taken out. I had these great dreams of changing, but perhaps this would just turn out to be a fantasy. With so many dangerous enemies all around and with a greatly diminished defence structure in place, would I survive? Only God could answer that question.

CHAPTER 14
ON MY WAY TO THE OUTSIDE

The money situation was vastly improving as time went by. First, I paid off the bad debt which was thousands of dollars, then I worked off all my fines and reparation simply by going to community work four days a week until it was all done. I completely paid off my mother before tidying up every small amount of money I knew of that I still owed. My credit rating was good by the time I had finished. After a few years back in town I had two cars, a Buell (road bike which is a sports frame with a Harley Davidson engine in it), I had a 2009 Triumph Bonneville and quite a bit of money on hand most of the time. I was doing well and I could have made a lot more if I had wanted to. I could have doubled, tripled or quadrupled my income, but I did not want to expand. I was aiming to get my finances in order and then I would quit and carry on with study. I genuinely wanted to be on that clean pathway to real life. I wanted to be out of this existence and into that place where no matter where you go there is hope. If you ask, "why would you want to give up a lot of money to go and study?" then I can tell you that it is an easy answer. Because now I genuinely believed in a Higher Power. I had seen the life lived by my friends and I, the other clubs and crews around New Zealand, and I had heard about and read about the different mobs around the world. Then I had seen the lives of individuals. I had taken so much in over time through reading and watching and listening that I just concluded that there was such a thing as good and evil. Through the use of drugs, the involvement in debauchery and violence, I had become aware of something that nobody has any explanation for, an evil that you can't even explain. I knew it was there. The evil and the darkness existed without a doubt. So, as they say, "The shadow proves the light". Where there is darkness there must be light.

My time in the life I had previously led was nearing its end and even though I had committed to change and to pursuing the light, I was still pulled down by circumstances around me and the fear that as I pulled out of the crew, I would become nothing. I had fought my entire life so that no one would be able to put me down but as time went by, I realised that no matter how much you fought, there would always be more fights. You could demolish a hundred guys or two hundred and no matter what there would always be more coming. You do not ever get to the end of the list. That is just the way the world works, there will always be people wanting to fight. What we must learn is how to avoid those fights. How to live a life where you are not around those types of people. If you do come across them at work or out in the world, you need to have ways to deal with them that are constructive and not destructive. There is a fine line that needs to be walked moving forward which was to maintain individual strength but also not revert to violence.

I knew this new path was the correct path to take, but it would not be easy. Instances would keep coming up whereby I felt as if I had no other choice but to stand my ground. I was in the process of learning different strategies and methods. Although the changes were picking up in pace it still was not happening overnight. Like all things the process would take time. Some of the last few instances that spring to mind were not necessarily in the exact order of how they took place but I do know that these last instances were in the final stretch. There would be another seven or eight events that took place as my time in that life came to an end. One of them was when I knocked over my sister's boyfriend one Christmas day. I also knocked over another one of my friends one day at his house. I do feel bad about that one, but I would suggest that this incident was linked to the problems going on between myself and Uncle. Again, I felt as though I had been betrayed and I was unequipped at this time to deal with the situation in a better way. I knocked over one of my neighbours on the other side of the street from me after I had confronted them about their music and one of them had become aggressive. That was unfortunate but it turned out okay a week later when he came over to apologise and we resolved our issues. Our young friend Neil also had some problems with a North Island gang member who had attempted to intimidate him. He came to me for assistance and of course I went around to his house knowing that this gang guy in question would soon be arriving. I know I should not have been getting involved but I just could not watch this young guy getting trampled on when all we had to do was flex a few muscles and back him up. The sergeant-at-arms arrived at the same time I did, and we waited for these guys to turn up which they did soon after. I was going to go straight out onto the street and take this gang guy on before he even had a chance to step foot in the property. As soon as I saw their car approaching, I pretended like I was a bit of a crazed guy and leaned against the fence and urinated. It was my way of letting them know they were in the wrong part of the country, plus at the same time I wanted to be comfortable before I took this guy on. The sergeant-at-arms stood and watched as I finished what I was doing and fixed my eyes on the opponents who were getting out of the car. Neil and one other guy also stood and waited for me to make a move. So, I moved towards them, gave them the signal that it was me verses the big guy and then walked out through the gate onto the tar seal where we would get down to business. The second gang guy who was there, had caused half the problems, but assumed as soon as he saw me that his friend would win and so leaned back on the bonnet of the car in attempt to suggest that the fight was already over. The big one came at me launching a couple of big hay makers which under normal circumstances would have won the fight for him. This time that was not to be the case, I only had to make a slight adjustment to my stance and these missiles were completely useless. Then it was my turn to advance on him and in the split second it took for his attempts to miss and my manoeuvre to begin he realised that I was about to eat him up and he suddenly started to reverse out of the danger that he was in. I stepped towards him, and he started reversing fast. Then, his accomplice who he was with realised they were in trouble, the car sprung into life and he started pulling away whilst signalling to the big guy. I did not even have to throw a punch and these two guys knew that they needed to move along fast, which they did.

Over the next couple of days, I did a night shift or two watching out for these guys in case they came back with numbers, but they never did. We were prepared if they did come back; it certainly would not have worked out well for them if they had. The final incident occurred when I ran into the big one in the supermarket a while later. I asked him if he wanted to finish it now that it was just me and him alone. To my surprise this big North Island gang guy turned down my offer.

The biggest event that brought our crew to an end was the fall out between the sergeant-at-arms and me. You see, I still got along fine with most of the older, original members of the club but they were not involved with our own crew which we put together in the years that followed the original club. Only some of the original members had joined with us and these were the guys that I was starting to fall out with. To this day I am still on good terms with most of the original members, but friendships with the likes of Uncle and the sergeant-at-arms turned sour as I began to make moves to get out. I recall the sergeant-at-arms becoming aggressive towards me on two separate occasions prior to the last time I visited him. On both occasions his character changed completely as if he was having an engine failure of the mind. After all we had been through together, after we had lived under the same roof at the clubhouse and various other properties, after the numerous times we had backed each other up, after Terry Brown had been taken out by unknown assailants while the sergeant-at-arms was in prison, after the fifteen years we had been friends and accomplices. Now, now he decides to treat me like I was beneath him! I could not believe it. He threatened me twice prior to my last visit and then on my final visit our conversation started like any other conversation but soon turned to some bizarre conspiracy he had concocted whereby he thought I was talking with Terry Brown. This was the drugs talking and I gently tried to tell him that this was just paranoia, but he exploded at me and jumped out of his seated position and proceeded to charge towards me. He was getting really wound up and as I was already standing at the front door I stepped outside and gave him some space to cool down. I really liked this guy you must understand. He had been my big brother for many years and, if any of us were given the respect of being an unofficial boss, it was him. Everyone just gave him space and respect and freedom to be who he wanted to be. Nobody questioned him really. To add to that he was one of our most feared hard men. Even the Harris gang would give him respect and stay out of his way. I saw it one time when we were up at the hospital together. Everyone paid respect to our sergeant-at-arms, and I certainly did as well. That is up until now. This suddenly became a very fragile moment because if we started something now, it would never end. I knew I could probably take him out, but should I? That was the question. If I did, our friendship was over for good simply because both of us were the same and once one of us succumbed to the other, we would become enemies for the rest of our lives. There was no doubting that. I had to make a split-second decision before it came to a head and my decision was to move towards the car without backing down and just do it in a way that was calm and relaxed and prevented the situation from getting any worse. I got in on the driver's side as he continued to hurl abuse at me through the window and that very second there, I knew we were done. We were going to fight, and our friendship was finished for good. To add to the seriousness of this situation there were other people inside the house who were listening. That as far as I was concerned was a major sign of disrespect and another example of what not to do when attempting to maintain a presence as a force to be reckoned with, because if people see or hear that your guys are not tight then that is a sign of weakness. Him going off at one of his own brothers was a sign of weakness and he could not even see it.

His flurry of abuse came to an end, and he walked off inside the house, so I started the car and slowly reversed out of the driveway and onto the street. As I drove away, I pondered what had just happened and of course what I would do about it. A sensation came over me which would best be described as a sadness or emptiness. For a man like me though it is impossible to allow those feelings to gain any stronghold. In my mind a man of strength must resist any temptation to fall into a state of victimhood. I now had to deal with this situation, and I had to come out on top, otherwise in my mind I would be allowing myself to be dominated which could not possibly happen. I had to be dominant in this situation. Not long after I rang the sergeant-at-arms, and I told him that what he had done was unacceptable and that we were no longer friends or brothers. I said, "That's it, you cannot behave like that towards me." I made it clear that our friendship was over. He agreed as if it was nothing to him and that was the end of the phone call. He obviously did not believe me and thought that within a few weeks we would be back to friends again; he just did not realise what he had done.

Some time would pass before we came face to face again. I saw the sergeant-at-arms in the aisles of the supermarket at the 24/7 shopping centre off Linwood Ave. I stared straight at him and I assumed he had seen me. As I moved along, I immediately thought about confronting him outside. I had been waiting for this moment, contemplating how I would get him and attempting to assess the dangers I might face as I went about it. But I knew that there was only one way to face another man of conflict in a way that would not bring unwanted criticism and possibly retaliation. That strategy was the same strategy that I always tried to use where it was possible. The one-on-one approach, step a man out one-on-one in a fair fight and what grounds for retaliation does he have? The answer is not a lot. In many of my fights, I used this approach because it put an end to a nasty situation in the most respectful manner. No knives, no guns, no two on one, nothing nasty which hopefully gives way to a resolution. Give a man the opportunity to fight his way out of a situation and he will retain his dignity whether he wins or loses; treat him like a dog and he will hate you forever.

Why did I need to go through with it? Because I was not fully saved yet, and I believed that if I left him as the dominant person then he would always have the upper hand. The sergeant-at-arms walked out the front doors of the supermarket as I sat in my car in the early hours of the morning. I had purposefully parked close enough to the entrance that he would see me as he walked out which he did. As soon as he saw me, I could tell he was not expecting any disturbance. He obviously thought I would not have the courage to take him on, as was the case with ninety nine percent of the people that ever came up against him. Everyone feared him due to his intimidating presence and hardened exterior. As he approached the vehicle he grinned as if nothing had changed, and we were about to have another catchup but that was the last thing on my mind. I wound down the window and the first thing he said was, "How's it going?"

My response was straight to the point, "I've already told you man, we're not friends anymore and I do not want anything to do with you, so there is no point coming up to talk to me".

In a typical challenging response he said, "What are you going to do about it?" That meant fight if you can, so it started just like that. It was his choice. He had the last say. I opened the car door as I positioned myself to exit the vehicle. Then I made my move pulling myself up. Suddenly he dropped his groceries on the ground and threw a punch as I was halfway out of the car but somehow, I dodged it and shoved the door open even further. I jumped in front of him as he threw another punch, this time a heavy haymaker, but his momentum was such that he literally spun himself around, so he was facing away from me. This gave me all the opportunity I needed so I slammed my fist into the back of his head. Following the head strike I came up behind him, put him in a choker hold and swung him to ground as easily as I could have ever hoped for. He sat on his back side on the concrete pavement as I stood behind him with my arm still around his throat. I could have broken his neck perhaps had I rag dolled him, or I could have launched a full-scale attack on his head, but instead I restrained him and yelled in his ear. I told him he was an idiot and that he should have known better. I reminded him of who he was dealing with and if he should ever forget again then he should just think of this moment, then I gave him one final shake and let go. I seriously could have killed him in that moment, but I did not want to hurt him, I just wanted to dominate him which I did without even suffering so much as a scratch. He knew what I had just done, and I could see the look in his eyes, and I will remember that forever. He scrambled around in the carpark trying to pick up his groceries as a supermarket worker came running out into the car park to see what was going on. I was still standing over him and blasting him with abuse. Then I turned and walked away never to talk to him again. I saw him one more time after that about a year later at the 24/7 dairy on Ferry Road and he would not even look at me.

Over the last year or so that I was in Woolston I was a little more on edge than normal as my crew had now been reduced to a handful of people. I did not let anyone know, but there was not really a structure in place anymore and had anything happened to me, I do not think there would have been any come back on it. I personally could have raised a small force to retaliate if I had needed to, but I doubt anyone else would have done that for me, which meant if anything happened to me there was no come back. So, I fortified my apartment even more than it had been before and I kept a close eye on any possible unwanted activity going on around me. I was being more careful than ever and ready should anything have happened. I kept my business going during that last year and the money kept rolling in. Soon I would be ready to make a move, but I just had to time it right. I had a party in the neighbour's apartment one night and invited a lot of my close friends. I used the neighbour's apartment because I did not want people partying at my place and his was a little rougher and better set up for a lot of people drinking and moving around. A lot of the old friends arrived, and it was a good night and probably one of the last times many of us were all in one place together. A bit of a sad time I guess in hindsight, but hey, never a dwell on a thought like that for too long.

The last couple of incidents that I can remember taking place in Christchurch before my departure were a run in with a guy from church who stole a porn shop docket from my ex-girlfriend's house as we were packing up her stuff to send up North to where she had relocated. He also stole some meds out of the bathroom and did some other weird stuff that kind of played on my mind a bit. He was a massive six-foot guy with a heavy build, and I genuinely thought he was just trying to wind me up, so I cornered him at the address he was staying and gave him a couple to the jaw. The church was certainly not happy about it and that is another whole story which I can't really get into now but let's just say I was on the edge of transformation, and these were my last couple of hiccups before the change. Grace from humans is a rarity, but the grace I received from above would save my life and be everlasting. It cannot be bought and was given freely. Finally, the last incident which I can remember was I had a stand off with three guys at the same time. They had been put onto me by a third party and came at me as if I were in the wrong which I was not. There were two ex-gang guys of a different club to us and another supporter so these guys should have known what they were doing. Obviously, I knew better though because as soon as they approached me, I dominated them with a barrage of words basically rebuking them for their assumptions. I then stepped them out one at a time and suggested that if they had a problem with me then they should have delt with it through the appropriate channels instead of the way that they did. Its kind of comical now when I think back because they accepted my rebuke and left without any further altercation. I spoke to one of them months later and apparently, he was so annoyed at the guy who had organised it that he drove off and left him on the side of the road without any ride home.

Over the course of the final year, I met a girl that would be my girlfriend for a while. She was not such a bad person or anything, but she was not squeaky clean. Her life, like mine, had been full of ups and downs and at the time she met me she was certainly struggling with a few issues. She came to stay with me in Christchurch and then she rented an apartment in Riccarton for a while. The whole time we were together we were in a bit of tug of war between doing the right thing, as in attempting to follow our Christian faith, or doing what we thought was fun but we knew to be wrong. Basically, I was still making money, so I had access to everything and the pair of us misbehaved. On the bright side, when we parted ways after six months or so I suddenly had an incredible revelation. This revelation would perhaps have been even more of a substantial revelation than I had had years before. It would end up being a major game changer.

CHAPTER 15

SO IF THE SON SETS YOU FREE, YOU WILL BE FREE INDEED. JOHN 8:36

What I believed was that there was a God. The same God that the Bible talks about and the same one that we learnt about in school and Sunday school years before. I had seen so much in this world ranging from very dark evil through to amazing, wonderful light, that I could no longer deny that there was something going on in our world. There was certainly a spiritual aspect to the world and, although I did not have all the answers yet, I certainly believed. The revelation that suddenly came to me was that for God to help me I needed to be within the bounds of His will for my life. For example, God has a will or a preferred plan for our lives, yet if we travel outside of that will, or preferred plan, then we are moving in a direction away from what God has in store for us. In the same way if we are moving in the direction of His will then surely any good He may have been planning for our lives will be inherited. Or to put it another way if you move in the realm of darkness then some of that realm will rub off on us and, likewise, if you make the conscious effort to walk in the light and follow the path outlined by God then you can rest assured that more good will come your way than bad.

From that moment on I wanted to be in the prepared path of God's will. Leading up to my split with my girlfriend I had been thinking along these lines and so a few weeks prior to our split I had completely dismantled my business. As I said this business was worth a lot of money and had I expanded it I could have made four times as much but even in the form that it was in it was a big earner. I could just feel this immediate need to dismantle the business and get on the right track. A lot of guys will keep going until they get caught or something goes wrong, but I stopped with absolutely no barrier in my way had I wanted to continue. So, in a way I felt quite good about myself because I gave up before I got stopped, I gave up from my own free will, and it was a choice based on principle and the desire to do the right thing. I went to my girlfriend at the time and told her that I had dismantled the business and I was startled when she told me I had done the wrong thing. I was really surprised, and I guess that was an indication that this woman was not heading in the same direction as me. She may have claimed to be thinking along the same lines as me, but I really don't think she was. But this did not phase me. I did not care what she thought, and I had already done it anyway. The business was well and truly shut down with no way of resurrection. Now I was going to be walking in the path of righteousness and as far as I was concerned nothing would stop me from now on.

One of the first things I did was head into the bush for several days to get away from everything and do some tramping. While I was in there, I came across one of the landowners who gave me a job straight away. Basically, I had an immediate out from the city. What a great start. I kept my apartment in the city and would travel in and out on the weekends. Employed as a fencer I worked some big hours which also helped financially. Things were going great for about the first five months as I worked during the week and went to church on the weekends. I could really feel myself making some good ground. The problem was though that the old life, and the old friends were only an hour's drive away. It was just too easy to fall back in with the same crowd and the same harmful activities if I was not careful. A couple of times I went back into town and hung out with Uncle and a few of the others. I just realised that gee, this was an incredibly difficult cycle to break. This was going to be harder than I thought. Then one day I was out on the High-Country station working away as per normal on a Monday morning and to be honest I do not think I was having a particularly good day prior to my revelation. But then it came to me in a flash. I knew now what I was going to do, I knew how I would break this cycle and do what very few other people have been able to do. I was going to go away, far away to a different country, and volunteer there and do something incredible. You see, up until now I had this idea where I would simply stay in New Zealand, give up the life and grind my way to a better future through the avenue of hard work and discipline. But this idea to be perfectly honest seemed quite boring to me. How could a guy like me who had lived the life then suddenly transform overnight into a boring stay at home guy? That is when I realised that I was on the right track because I needed something fantastic and exciting to do to replace what I had before. I needed something way better, I needed an extreme adventure.

This was to be the perfect adventure. In the space of a few hours, I came up with the idea. I had heard of a country called Sierra Leone which was on the West Coast of Africa in-between Guinea and Liberia. I knew nothing of this country at first other than it was in a song that I liked sung by a band named Coconut Rough. The song was called *Sierra Leone*. All I knew was that it was some crazy rough place on the other side of the world where you might die if you were not lucky. I really did not care; the name was so alluring and beautiful and I literally fell in love with this plan straight away. Years later I would find out that Sierra Leone is the place where the movie *Blood Diamonds* with Leonardo DiCaprio is set. But I certainly did not know that back then when I first came up with the idea. I remember going in at lunch time and sitting with the new manager of the station and the whole lunch break I was just glowing on the inside because I had an amazing plan that was going to take me away on this great adventure. I never told anyone at work or my old friends. I kept it to myself because I did not want this plan spoilt. The only person I told at first was my friend from church who was a lawyer. His name was John Wilks and he immediately said to me that yes that is a great idea but first you need to pray about it and get solid confirmation that this is a good idea, and then you need to go to Bible college before you set off. I thought about what he said, and I agreed. Firstly, confirmation for those of you who do not know is basically praying and waiting for supernatural confirmation that what you want to do is the will of God and not just some idea that you have come up with on your own. So that part was easy I thought, and I would do as he suggested and just see what came of it. The second part, going to Bible college was doable too I imagined. Let us get on with it I thought and see what we can come up with. The first thing I did was pray in Church one Sunday for confirmation. My exact prayer was, "Can I go to Sierra Leone?" The second I finished praying I opened my Bible and it fell open on the first page of the book of Jonah. This is called the open book confirmation technique where you let the Bible fall open and read where your eyes land. This is a controversial technique because obviously people might often get the wrong answer but for me, a complete beginner, I thought it was an okay way to start. So, my eyes landed on the first verse in the book of Jonah which reads as follows:

Jonah 1 verse 1 The word of the Lord came to Jonah son of Amittai: 2 "Go to the great city of Nineveh and preach against it, because its wickedness has come up before me."

That was the scripture that I read immediately after praying and that was good enough for me. I mean there is a lot of pages in the Bible and a lot of different scriptures and for me to rest my eyes straight away on something that says that, well, let us just say that you could not really ask for a better confirmation verse when asking whether or not you can go somewhere. I thought it was perfect anyway and I took that as a yes.

The next step was going to Bible college, as recommended by my friend John. It made sense to do this because I needed to iron out a few of my issues and refine my personal character before I headed away. Obviously, that was going to be a big job in itself due to the way I had lived my life but certainly not unachievable. Prior to all this happening I had already been baptised, I had been through a couple of different church programmes including the "Breaking of the iniquities and generational attachments" programme, and finally some one-on-one mentoring with Fons van Wamel who had been running the iniquities course with his wife Cathy. So, basically, I had done a certain amount of personal development already before I left but there was still a lot to do. The other line of thought which I agreed with was the idea that through my time at college I would be able to make connections in Sierra Leone before I went. Missionary connections perhaps, or connect with an existing organisation over there who could help facilitate my arrival and long-term stay. That was the idea anyway.

First on the list of things to do though was to tidy up all my loose ends, enrol in college and then head away and get into it. In hindsight everything went smoothly. By mid-2011 I had started my Diploma in Christian Ministry at Lifeway College in Snell's Beach, Warkworth. Founded some years ago by a small group of Christians led by evangelist and entrepreneur, Trevor Yaxley, the college offered courses in business and animation, in addition to Christian ministry. This made for a varied campus body. I had found out about it from two visitors who came to a homegroup I had been attending.

It sounded like a lot of fun and after some consideration I decided Lifeway would be the best option for me because I could start almost straight away. Other Bible colleges, such as Laidlaw, had a lot more application requirements and different intake dates. Another great aspect about my choice was that it was well away from Christchurch, which would have the added benefit of immediately detaching me from my old life. This would be like an immediate divorce from my old life rather than a problematic slow gradual separation. Another plus about Lifeway was that it was surrounded on two sides by farmland which would make it fairly easy to find work.

I had let my rented apartment out to another guy who was going to pay the rent while I was away and basically took most of my important stuff with me. The plan was to go and if possible, not come back, but it was handy to still have access to this flat should I need it at a later stage. I sold both of my bikes, the Triumph and the Buell, and I also sold the nicer of my two cars keeping only the practical station wagon as an A to B vehicle which I imagined I would definitely need. What money I had accumulated from the activities I had been involved with and the sale of my vehicles really didn't last too long once the inflow came to a halt and by the time I left Christchurch it would be fair to say I had broken even. I'd paid the big debts I had wanted to clear like the one to my mother and the various other commitments including the cost of shifting up North, but really from this time forward I was putting my faith in God. My finances were now in His hands, and I trusted that what I would have come in would be enough to see me through. So, I arrived in Snell's Beach ready for study and we were into it straight away. The other students had started at the beginning of the year, but it really didn't matter that I was starting halfway through the year because the Diploma was made up by credits. The idea was that I would just finish later and if I met the required amount of time in class and passed in all the different topics then I was good to go. Although this Diploma only ran for one year it was a very time-consuming programme with as many as sixty hours per week including serving, hence the short one year turn around. Basically, we were cramming a two-year course into one year. The course revolved around military style fitness training first thing in the morning to develop discipline and then from 8:30am onwards, Monday to Friday, we would be in classroom lectures or being tutored. So, it was 6:00am training, then breakfast, classroom during the day and then training again at 4:30pm, five days a week. Often when we were doing camps or challenges or serving at conferences, we would go right through the weekend too which would really bulk out the hours that we were doing. Also, most of us had to serve in some way or another at the campus church service on the Sunday, although I avoided some of this requirement since I was also working a part time job on the Saturday, which meant Sunday was my only day of rest.

So, that was my life. I was extremely busy, but living in the beautiful beachside town of Snell's Beach far away from the old life I knew. I was surrounded by Christians and people with a completely different perspective on life than I had ever experienced before. Some of these people were awesome. Looking back ten years later at this moment in time I realise now that this was the moment when I was truly free. I didn't know it at the time because of course I still had all these anxieties and fears going on in my mind, but I can now see that from that moment on I was set free from my old life. Yes, I would still face some struggles in the future, they are a fact of life, but the reality is that unbeknown to me my life was truly on track now for a better future.

John 8:36
So if the son sets you free, you will be free indeed.

CHAPTER 16

THE BEGINNING OF MY NEW LIFE

My time at Bible College went by very fast and before long I was nearing the end of my first six months. I really do need to thank those
guys and ladies up there in Snell's Beach who helped me through
that first six months of my new life. Pete Meafou, the senior College tutor
and Pastor Reuben Gwyn were both amazing in their roles. Both guys
were very positive and never let me down the entire time I was involved
with them. Pete was such a solid guy and Reuben Gwyn continues to have
answers to those difficult questions every time I talk to him, which is still
on a regular basis. Christina Wylie, in her role as the College Registrar and
her husband, Caleb, our Life Group Leader and friend were awesome people to have around during this time. I made numerous other friends during
my time at Snell's Beach.

Life was good despite the usual bumps along the way. It was at the end
of this first six months that a group of seven of us went on a two-and-a-
half-week mission trip to the Philippines. Six students and the second tutor
Grace Presland–White all went to meet up with the founder and director
of Global Impact, which is a non-profit organisation serving the needs of

the people in the Philippines and the Ukraine. This was my first overseas trip and what an amazing time it was. I saw first-hand what life was like outside the normality of the structured country that I had been brought up in. The Philippines is a developing country, and more than a hundred million people live there spread out over a series of islands in a part of the world known as Southeast Asia. Until you have been there you just cannot comprehend what it will be like, what the people will be like. As a part of the preparation for what I wanted to do in the future this had to be one of the most inspiring and educational aspects of my entire journey. As they say, God is good and I can only attribute this good fortune to the Almighty one who opened the doors for me. I cannot recall now exactly where all the money came from, but I am positive it was no coincidence that this money, which came from various people and circumstances, just happened to arrive all at the same time right when I needed it for this trip.

After the Philippines trip, the year came to an end relatively quickly. The summer break was upon us, and it was time to make some decisions about what I would do. Of all the trials I had encountered during that first six months of freedom I believe the hardest part for me was learning to deal with people again. Yes, I had some wonderful support and new friends now, but I struggled to fit in with the students and this had an impact on me as I believe I took it personally. Ten years on, having the benefit of hindsight, I think that the years I spent around the club sheltered me in a way where I never had to learn how to deal with people and all I knew previously was how to cut them off. This didn't work when I was forced to live around people 24/7 and so began the learning curve which I look back on and am thankful for. Now I know that this is just a part of life. Wherever you go you will always find challenging people and you have just got to keep going, keep positive and keep praying for these people. It's the only way and most importantly, do not take it personally.

So as the summer break began, I made the decision to go back to Christchurch to work for one of my old bosses on the farm just for a couple of months to earn some extra dollars. Yes, it was a dangerous decision to make and possibly not the right one but, in the end, it turned out fine. I worked hard right through the summer break and was able to meet up with Fons once again to really thrash out some of that important mentoring that I was probably in need of before the final trip back up North. Fons and I discussed some issues in those final few meetings that I believe set the foundation for success. In amongst the newfound freedom of college and my new life these last few hours I spent with him in prayer and devotions really made something shift that to this day has never been reversed. Approximately ten years later in the year 2021 I can tell you now that the year of 2011 was a majorly significant year for me not only in freedom from the old life but everything about the old life. The drugs, the woman, the violence, the debauchery. In the year of 2011 everything changed and there is only one feasible explanation for how this could have happened, and that explanation is the presence of the Almighty One.

I returned to Snell's Beach after the holidays ended and resumed my studies at the college. It was great to be back, and I was looking forward to the adventures that were to come. Around this time or not long after, the guy who was looking after my rental in Christchurch finally moved out and so I had no option but to close that door on that part of my life. I was now well and truly living in the North Island, and this was now my permanent base. I was living on the college campus, and I had five months left of study before I would start working full time and preparing to head overseas to the great country of Sierra Leone where I intended to serve as a volunteer. That was still my main goal and a major driving force to keep me on track. I knew that this adventure to Africa had to happen. For now, this plan was my biggest dream and hope for the future. This was such a driving force for me that I was fearful of ever doing anything against the will of God in the fear that I might lose this great opportunity, and it worked. I remained on track. So many of my thoughts were devoted to working out how this would happen and how I could be the best I could possibly be in my lead up to this journey. A lot of hard work went into this project, hours upon hours of personal counselling and training with Pastor Reuben Gwyn, and endless emails and phone calls to people, some I never even knew before, in the hope that this plan would all come together in the end. This was not an easy option as far as mission destinations normally go but I had the passion and the motivation to make this happen and I would not stop until it was done.

Over 2012 some reasonably major events unfolded. LIFE, the church which at the time owned and operated Lifeway College, planned a two-and-a-half-week mission trip to Cambodia which I was invited to go on. Pastor Reuben was to be the leader of the mission and I think about eleven others including myself made up the rest of the team. Yet again this was an incredible turn of events which saw me managing to raise the funds for this trip. It was most definitely uncanny how it unfolded. I really didn't think I had enough to go but I had committed to the trip on the basis that I would try my hardest to raise the funds, but if it did not work out, I could easily pull out giving the others time to go ahead without me. One weekend I thought that the New Zealand Warriors were supposed to be playing a game. I had arranged to watch the game with a friend at a local restaurant in Warkworth and I headed down there to find a seat early, only to realise when I got there that I had mixed up the days. I quickly messaged my friend to alert him to my mistake and then pondered what my next move would be. I then started talking to a complete stranger. He was a guy, who I think had been raised around the area, but had spent a lot of time recently down in Christchurch working on the rebuild after the significant

earthquake which had damaged many areas in the city. I think his name
was Daniel. After the usual introductions, the conversation moved onto
what I was doing and where I wanted to be in the near future. I told him
about Sierra Leone and about our upcoming trip to Cambodia. Daniel
immediately offered to contribute money towards the mission and within a
few days he had deposited nearly two thousand dollars into my account. I
could hardly believe it. Completely blew me away and this money basically
topped up the exact amount that I needed. So, to summarise what happened, I went to watch a game that wasn't even on at a restaurant, began
talking to a stranger and he gives me two thousand dollars towards my
mission trip. Wonders do happen.

Over the years that would follow many wonders such as this would
be delivered. I began to realise that God had my back no matter what
happened. I could rely on Him, and he would not let me down. The
Cambodia trip was another amazing time away. The twelve of us provided
approximately twelve hundred hours of labour over a ten-day period to the
Cambodian New Life Fellowship. They had a few major centres in Phnom
Penh and hundreds of smaller groups throughout the regions where they
held regular services, but it was at the main centre of New Life Fellowship
in Phnom Penh where the twelve of us spent our ten days renovating and
upgrading. After the ten days of work, we all had about four days of spare
time to explore and enjoy ourselves. While the rest of the guys went out
to the beaches and to some of the major sightseeing destinations, I stayed
in Phnom Penh and became better acquainted with some of the New Life
Fellowship staff and locals. I had an awesome time and even got to talk
with some of the guys involved in the anti-trafficking programmes and the
like.

2012 had another significant event take place which I am proud to
report on. I completed my Diploma in Christian Ministry and was given

an Award of Academic Excellence at the graduation ceremony which took place sometime later. The reason I received this is because out of ten modules I had nine A+ grades and one A. The modules we studied were: Personal Development, Spiritual Growth, Leadership, Ministry Skills Development, Preparation for Ministry, Theology, Biblical Interpretation, Evangelism 1 and 2, and World View. I am so grateful for the time I spent at Lifeway College and nearly every day that goes past since I finished at Lifeway I will remember and utilise some of the teaching I was blessed with during this period of time.

After I completed the Diploma, I remained on campus for some time and went on to be employed by the college as part of the maintenance team under the quiet direction of the Property Manager and Christian role model, Malcom Collier. I remained as a member of the Church and in the midst of preparing for my next overseas expedition I attempted to retain the strong bond between myself and the other members of the church and college community that I had become familiar with. For a while there I was working about four different jobs including the college maintenance job in my attempt to put together enough funds for my overseas expedition. All was going well and there was nothing I could see standing in the way of me and my Sierra Leone. I would make it even if it killed me in the long run. I really did not care, I just had to make it there. It was a goal that had to be accomplished.

2012 and my new life beginning unfortunately did not only bring good fortune. This is a reality of life; with the good you must also take the challenges. To accompany the success of the Cambodia trip and the Award of Academic Excellence there were trials I was facing along the way and I think it is fair to say that some of these challenges may be lifelong ones. You see, it's easy for people to think that a guy like myself can walk away from a life of sin unscathed and walk happily off into the sunset. This may happen in some instances but often it doesn't happen like that. In my case, I think there was a certain amount of sunset but also there were difficulties that I had to face. Residue of the old life and complications don't always get resolved overnight. I spent half my life fighting and standing up against what I believed were evil people, only to realise that every time I won or stood up against a crew of guys, I found myself with even more enemies than before. So, I started off with a small number of enemies and by the time I finished I had enemies in a lot of different corners of Christchurch and even New Zealand. To this day there are guys out there who don't like me. Don't get me wrong, there are occasions where a fair gentlemen's fight took place and we've become friends afterwards. There are even groups of guys whose hearts have changed over time, but in many cases people just can't let go of their hurt. A lot of the time in the eyes of the ones who came off second best, I or we, became the 'bad guys'. Because of this phenomenon I have people out there that, given the chance would try and pull down any progress that I make. This has happened along the path of my journey and no doubt will continue to happen in the future. There have been instances where undoubtably guys have spread false accusations and negativity about me. There may have been a little bit of that going on up North and on the odd occasion in the years that followed, but the key is to stay positive and not let yourself be distracted by such things. It's good to keep moving forward and have faith that God can take all things, even the bad things, and turn them around for the betterment of us all.

Regardless, I am happy to reiterate my gratitude to God for the wonderful things he did in my life while I was up North and again my gratitude to the supportive friends that helped me out so much when I was up there. It was a great time and a great learning curve. 2013 would be my final year in Snell's Beach and I spent the entire year preparing for my expedition to Sierra Leone. In my final year I was mainly off the college campus, but still

THE BEGINNING OF MY NEW LIFE

very involved with the church and community. I even became involved with the youth group for a month or two because I was certain that the experience I gained would be invaluable overseas, which it was. It is quite amazing how it all eventually came together in the end; so many different people played out varying roles. Just the slightest little tip like the use of a particular website for bookings may seem insignificant but in the long run potentially saved me thousands. And that was just a simple suggestion from a decent guy who turned out to be a big help. Then came the financial supporters that believed in me enough to contribute money and prayer support. I had also made connections in Sierra Leone via advice given through the college tutor Pete Meafou. Everything was now set up and ready to go, so I booked my tickets for January 2014 with the intention of staying eight months as a starter. What an amazing time this was going to be and although I was very anxious about everything going to plan, I think I had this quiet confidence that I was in safe hands. The fact that I only had one contact and that Sierra Leone was a country with a dangerous reputation could have put some people off, but for me I was drawn to this uncertainty. I felt good about doing something that others might shy away from.

CHAPTER 17

SIERRA LEONE

January 2014 rolled around quickly and before long I was saying my goodbyes to everyone and boarding a plane that would connect me with several other planes which would eventually after a near thirty hours of flying land me in Sierra Leone. And land in Sierra Leone I certainly did. We came down on the tarmac and for me it was with a rush of adrenalin and excitement. Apart from the transit in Nairobi, Kenya, on the way over I had never before stepped foot on the continent of Africa. And here I was about to experience for the first time the country that I had been dreaming about for the past several years. We had descended towards the airport through thick cloud. Once we were on the tarmac all I could see was green jungle-like growth down the sides of the runway. The airport itself was quite small and as we neared the entrance after exiting the plane, I could see long grass growing up through the cracks in the concrete. This immediately signified that there was no fancy setup and yes, I was in Africa. The waves of heat penetrated my clothing to the point where I felt like I was standing in a sauna. I had to pass through multiple security checkpoints and luggage inspections before I was finally allowed out of the airport. What a feeling it was to be finally allowed out through those doors and into the adventure of my lifetime. My contact, James, stood there waiting as I exited the building. We greeted each other enthusiastically and made our way to where the taxis were waiting. Even the taxis were a sight to see, as apart from being painted in the traditional taxi yellow colour, not much else about them resembled a normal taxi. The windows were broken or even non-existent, some had their boots tied down with string, and they were banged and dented like they'd been through a tough life. This was so different and, to be honest, exactly what I had been hoping for.

There were people everywhere and man it felt good to be amongst them. The main language in Sierra Leone is Krio, an English-based Creole, similar to a Pidgin English. Of course, there are numerous other languages that are spoken in Sierra Leone as well, for instance every different tribe in Sierra Leone has its own language. Many Sierra Leoneans are multilingual, able to speak Krio, their tribal language and, if they have been through the education system, often they can speak English as well. This made it reasonably easy for me to communicate with James and many of the other Sierra Leoneans I was soon to become acquainted with.

We caught a taxi from the airport to the ferry and then caught the ferry across from Lungi to where the capital city Freetown lay. Entering Freetown for the first time was an amazing experience that I will never forget. I realise many other people have also been inside developing countries, or at least viewed the footage of developing countries, and this is helpful because in a way you can get some sort of an idea of what it is like in a place like Freetown. But nothing can ever match being there in person. Its only then that you can really understand what it is like. Even for me to explain the situation is not an easy task because there are just so many intricate details about such a place that I could just go on forever. But I guess a good starting point would be to mention some aspects of the country, for instance nearing the end of the 1990's and the early 2000's Sierra Leone was considered one of the most dangerous countries in the world due to the horrific civil war which lasted for approximately eleven years. Well over fifty thousand people were killed in the war and according to some reports the number may have been a lot higher. Also, this is just an estimation of casualties, it does not include those that died from malnutrition, lack of medical care and the various other problems that arose throughout this drawn-out conflict. It's also estimated that half a million refugees fled to neighbouring countries and that over a million people were displaced internally. Large scale human rights violations were perpetrated throughout the duration of the war with most of the atrocities being carried out by members of the rebel RUF groups and their allies. The rebels perpetrated a campaign of shock and horror on the civilian population through the use of amputations and murder. No one was safe and the scars of this war remain long after the final shot was fired. No amount of writing or explanation can ever give credit to the substantial trauma inflicted on this country and its people. It is unexplainable.

Not long after the war ended, Sierra Leone became known as one of the most corrupt countries in the world. This probably contributed to it now being one of the poorest countries in the world. Poverty is widespread and large sprawling slums are commonplace in many parts of the country including Freetown. However, like any country varying levels of prosperity do exist. For example, in the wealthy areas of Freetown beautiful multi-storey homes grace the landscape. Then there is the middle of the range average income earners who manage to get by and build homes and a future for their children. Sierra Leone has all types but without a doubt no one can deny that this is a country where financial struggles affect most people. The poverty is clearly visible as soon as you step foot inside the country. From sparsely clad children selling produce in baskets atop their heads in the marketplace to amputees sitting on the side of the road begging for change, examples are in abundance. As soon as I got there, I could see it.

Sierra Leone is on the West Coast of Africa in-between Liberia and Guinea. It has a tropical climate with a wet season and a dry season and most of the countryside is ex-rainforest which has now become vast expanses of regrowth or palm trees. There are still significant areas of rainforest left in various parts of the country and isolated pockets of cultivated agricultural land in amongst the much larger areas of regrowth. During the dry season it doesn't rain at all for months at a time, but then gradually as the seasons begin to change the rains start to come sporadically until the peak of the wet season arrives and it's raining nearly every single day. When it rains in Sierra Leone it really rains. I have seen bathtub size containers filling up from the drains of a roof in a matter of seconds. Massive volumes of water can fall out of the sky and at times the water can become so much that it has caused significant problems for the inhabitants of the areas more vulnerable to flooding. This is real rain. Freetown is nestled in-between the hills of the Peninsula Mountains and the coastline of the Atlantic Ocean. This city has more than one million inhabitants who come from a variety of different backgrounds and cultures. Many are from the various tribal groups around the country such as the Mende, Koranko, Temne, and Limba tribes but there are also a group known as the Krios. The Krios are a multi-ancestral group who were originally freed slaves sent back to Africa and resettled in the area of Sierra Leone which they now call Freetown. Obviously, the name Freetown was influenced by the influx of these newly freed slaves. The Krios now make up a significant part of the Freetown population and in many cases have played a vital role in the country's development and successes. As far as the general population of Sierra Leone goes there is roughly eight million people and at a guess, I would say 80% are from the various tribal groups I mentioned. Then the remaining 20% is a mixture of different backgrounds such as Krios, Liberians, Guineans, and people from other parts of the world. There is a small Lebanese population in various parts of the country and people of Indian descent. Of course, there are a small number of Westerners in Sierra Leone, but not a huge number. All these people make up the wonderful part of the world where those of us that have travelled or lived there come to love.

That evening on the first day we drove through Freetown heading out of town on a busy road packed with other vehicles, especially motorbikes. The bikes were everywhere and there were thousands of them. Something that I would become very familiar with over time. We made a couple of stops as we left Freetown and one of those stops ended up being at a Pharmacy that sold medicines and drugs. I had never seen anything like this before in my life. Not even in the Philippines or Cambodia did it appear to be this rough. We parked outside the drug store and one of the occupants of the vehicle got out and made his way upstairs to an apartment above the drug store. I looked around outside the jeep and there were broken down car wrecks sitting on their rims parked outside the store with long grass growing up around them and covered with dust. It appeared as if everything was covered with dust: the windows in the stores, the signs, the cars, the tarpaulins draped around the place and even the car I was sitting in was partially covered in filth. I guess this is to be expected when so many of the roads in and around Freetown are either dirt or in poor condition. I quickly noticed that most of the doors and windows on the buildings and houses were protected by steel shutters or bars. Obviously some of the tin shacks didn't have this feature but the more permanent buildings did. This kind of protection is normally standard procedure when building in Sierra Leone unless you can't afford it. Another feature of many of the properties that I saw that night were the security fences. Large concrete block fences formed compounds around the residences within. Razor wire was draped in between the steel pillars holding them up along the top of the walls. Another observation were the shards of broken glass that had obviously been set in place on top of the block fences when the cement was still wet. This formed a formidable obstacle for any person attempting to scale the fences. I had never seen glass used like that before. Many of the fences were also made of corrugated iron or tin and were held up by bush sticks or poles cut out of the jungle. Obviously, these were not visually fantastic, but I could see how they formed some sort of privacy and protection for those that had constructed them. These were some of the scenes I was confronted with on my first night inside Sierra Leone, and as the engine of the jeep burst to life again and carried us away from the drug store, I wondered what else I would encounter as time went by.

We rumbled our way down the motorway out of Freetown for what seemed like a considerable amount of time passing an endless sea of block and tin buildings underneath the ever-darkening night sky. Occasionally bright lights would appear out of the darkness of congregation points for the Sierra Leoneans enjoying the night life but the further out we went from the city the less activity we encountered. The last major junction that we passed on the way out was a place called Tumbu Junction, but I had no idea where I was by this stage as we sped straight past on our way inland. Beyond Tumbu Junction the residences appeared to be spread out more and as we neared James's area the busy city life now seemed to be far behind us. This was still a residential area, but it had a quiet suburban feel about it, even a village atmosphere you could say. The jeep finally slowed and veered off the highway and through a dirt yard full off wrecked cars and tin shacks. Then as we continued through the pitch black of the night with only the head lights of the jeep, we pulled back onto another sealed road. After bouncing through potholes and past dimly-lit residences and small gatherings of locals on the side of the road we made another hard left and pulled onto yet another unsealed surface which turned out to be an entrance into the network of dirt roads around where James lived. As we bounced through very deep potholes toward the intersection of the road James's house was on, I peered into the darkness and was able to make out long grass everywhere and what appeared to be unfinished block buildings that were completely overgrown. This was really getting to be some journey and, as I think back I remember I was void of any fear. Absolutely no fear at all. Some might find that hard to believe considering the history of the country to date, but I know that this is true. I believed God had brought me to this country for his own special purpose and I believed nothing could touch me. If I remained within God's will then I would remain within his protection. Even if I made a mistake I would remain within his protection. It would only be if I deliberately walked away from Him and put my body into unsanctioned places would I risk being outside of God's protection and I can tell you right now that I had no intentions of doing that, especially in a place like Sierra Leone.

That night James's family welcomed me into their home for the first time and I felt very lucky to be there with them. James had a wife called Christiana and three children plus a grandson. They lived in a small three-bedroom block house with the garage attached. A generator was used for electricity and water had to be bucketed in from outside. I would soon learn that this kind of setup is widespread throughout Sierra Leone. I mean, this was standard. Nobody except a few who lived in the main cities had electricity sourced from a power company. Nearly everybody used a generator. Those that didn't have a generator would charge their appliances at a local charging centre, which was basically just a power generating property that was open to the public. Most water in Sierra Leone came from a well. Water was carried by buckets from a community well to the property where you stayed. If you were lucky enough to have a well on your property then that made things a little easier with only a short carry to the house. In some of the main cities there were government pipes supplying water to the public. I also heard that, especially during the dry season, these can dry up completely and people sometimes had to carry water for kilometres from other parts of the city. In the area where I would be staying which was at least an hour's drive from Freetown there was no power supply company and well water only, but that to me was no problem at all. Such a small challenge as this seemed like an insignificant price to pay for such a wonderful experience.

That night I had my first Sierra Leonean meal which was cassava leaf on rice, and I was able to spend a couple of hours getting to know James's family before we all retired for the night. All in all, it was a joyful and successful first day and everything went according to plan without any unforeseen problems. It was a great way to start my adventure. The next few weeks were full to the brim with activities right from the beginning. That's the way I wanted it. I really wanted to make good use of my time and keep busy the entire time. Afterall, there were people who had invested their money into this trip and I certainly wanted to make sure that everyone got their money's worth. Plus, for my own personal reasons as well. The different life experiences I had been through had helped to develop a good work ethic in me. By the time I ended up in Sierra Leone you could easily say that unless I was doing something constructive, I wasn't happy, that's just the way I was and even to this day I'm still like that to a certain degree. First, I had to get myself settled into the building where I would be living. This was about a kilometre from James's house and was an old two storey house which had been used for several years as a part time headquarters for various missionary groups and for housing associated people. In the downstairs, back corner of the house lived a couple who I soon got to know well. The house was very basic; water had to be brought in and electricity was supplied by a generator. Another daily issue was the mosquito problem. In Sierra Leone there is a lot of malaria, so you have to sleep under a mosquito net and take the necessary precautions to avoid catching it. Of course, then you must treat it once you do get it, unless you want to take malaria medication all the time which a lot of people aren't keen on doing. There are stories of people who lived up on the hill in the nicer suburbs of Freetown who hadn't had to deal with malaria, but I would suggest that they were probably just lucky to have been living over the side of town near the ocean where there weren't so many mosquitoes. The same British couple who told me about their experience later moved out to where I was living in the Western Rural District and immediately got sick from malaria which seems to confirm what I am saying. But anyway, I will touch more on the malaria subject a little later, because that really is a horrendous killer and it very nearly got me on one occasion.

Across the road from where I stayed was an orphanage run by an awesome man of God, the Reverend Hassan Mansaray, who has become a good friend. The orphanage originally started during the civil war so most of the children were grown up or in their teens by the time I arrived. There were a few younger ones there and to make use of the space they also had a few families associated with the church or orphanage living on site as well. The property itself was a great setup. A fully enclosed compound of approximately 8000 to 12000 square metres. Perhaps about two or three acres. This used to be an old hospital during the civil war and was later transferred to the orphanage. So, as I said it was a great setup with a solid security fence all the way around and strong, well-maintained facilities. It was here that I would fetch my water for the house as they had a well in the far corner of the compound and so over time, I became well acquainted with a number of these guys who are still friends. I became friendly with the younger guys first because they were the ones I interacted with daily while I lived across the road. They were the ones that helped fetch water for me when I first got sick with malaria. The Reverend Hassan Mansaray had founded this orphanage and another orphanage closer to Freetown. He has also planted approximately thirteen churches in Sierra Leone. One of these churches I attended near Freetown had a few hundred people present the day I was there. I know this church alone does a large amount of work in the community, so really I think my statement that this guy is a great man of God is quite true and I can certainly say that he is up there with the best of the guys that I met in Sierra Leone. Reverend Hassan will tell you God has done all the work and that he is just lucky enough to have been involved, which is also true, but I'd like to give credit where credit is due and I believe Reverend Hassan deserves some.

So as the first few weeks flew by, I got stuck in and did as much as I could. I established a routine and worked out how everything went including internet, banking, transport, and much more. I also went with James on a few trips into Freetown where I got a great look at the full extent of the inner city and its workings. Freetown surely has that big city feel about it in comparison to other parts of the country. You'll find the multi-storey buildings, banks, district courts, other government buildings, modern shops, the hustle and bustle and much more. It is the African version though, so for those that haven't been there before I would say you'd still be in for quite a surprise. For me I would say most of it was a pleasant surprise but of course as in the case of any newcomer you will generally find a few things that tend to make you a little uncomfortable. But that's just life, when you come from one culture, and you go to experience another some things take a little while to adjust to.

Prior to my arrival in Sierra Leone, I had planned to be involved with a group programme run by a Christian organisation which James was also involved with. However, it was unclear whether the group would still be going ahead as planned because there didn't appear to be the numbers required to proceed. For this reason, I had a few weeks up my sleeve while

we waited for a decision on the programme, so I decided to keep busy as
per usual and see what project I might be able to embark on. James and
his wife Cristiana had been involved with the planning and construction of
a small rural school about half an hour's drive from where we lived. After
an initial visit to the school, we decided that there was quite a bit of work
that I could do to assist in the development of the property. For a start, like
several of the developing countries that I have visited, they had a rubbish
problem. It was decided that I could dig a pit and then put in place a simple weekly procedure that the caretakers and staff could follow to keep the
grounds clean. I personally think that this very basic task of sorting out a
property's rubbish problem can have a tremendous impact not only on the
visual appeal of a site but also on the people that must work there every
day. How many of us would agree that resting at the end of a long week
in a tidy and clean house is much preferable than to try and 'kick back' in
a place littered with rubbish and dirty laundry? I think everybody would
agree with me that clean and tidy completely changes the atmosphere of
a place and makes it a lot more pleasant. So, to me it's no different when
you're walking through a school yard, a farmyard or a village- keep it tidy
as it makes a huge difference. A perfect example is that of a village. There
might be a small village by a river just a few kilometres off the main road
and perhaps there might be an opportunity for a bit of tourism or some
visitors who might like to add some value to the local market or even just
for the sake of the people that live there. Imagine the village in two separate
ways. Firstly, imagine if you walk through that village and all you can see is
plastic wrappers and bits of rubbish built up everywhere, on the sides of the
road, beside all the houses and buildings, and even in the communal areas.
I immediately think slum. Now walk through that exact same village and
the roads and the grounds and the communal areas are free from rubbish,
completely free because people have spent time each week cleaning up and

they have a system for putting that rubbish where it belongs. Now what do you think? I think beautiful rural African village. If I think that so will the tourists, so will the prospective investors and so will the people that wake up to it every morning. Granted, not everybody is equipped to think positive thoughts all the time, but I would say at least a good number of people who saw it would be a lot more positive about such a village if it was in the state that I just described. Even if it's just for the people that live there, a simple system can take them out of a slum and put them in a beautiful setting. That's the way I see it.

I understand there are much larger problems facing Sierra Leone and the rest of the world other than rubbish. For example in Sierra Leone we have the poverty problem, the corruption, the housing issues and the numerous life-threatening difficulties that Sierra Leoneans can face daily, but cleaning up is a small task which if managed correctly can take very little time and can create a better environment for all involved. That is why I like to encourage it and that's why when I live or work in a certain area, I take pride in trying to improve it. I dug that pit in those school grounds for James by hand on my own with a pick and a shovel. By the time I finished it was wide enough and deep enough to solve their garbage problem for some time. One afternoon, we sent everyone out and within an hour or two we had collected every piece of rubbish on the grounds. What a tremendous difference it made. In the space of a few hours that school went from looking like a school in the middle of a slum to a school in the beautiful wilds of Africa. So nice that you could pitch a tent in the middle of it and camp there for a week! Very satisfying. Over the course of the next few months, we dug a number of these pits in different locations around where I lived and worked and implemented systems where all of us played a part in keeping the environment clean and healthy.

Another task I agreed to go ahead with required the use of a chainsaw, a fair bit of gas and some blood, sweat and tears. Well perhaps not the tears but everything else for sure. The project included the expansion of the children's playing fields. They already had a dirt playing area in-between the classroom blocks, but that area did not expand far behind the classrooms and certainly not far enough to be big enough for a full-sized football field which is what they wanted. An area had been allocated for the field and some attempts had been made to clear some of the brush but the main obstacles still in the way were the extremely large palm trees that reached up into the sky. At least half a dozen of those trees remained in the way plus a small amount of vegetation. I was lucky enough to purchase a second-hand Husqvarna with a 16-inch bar in brand-new condition. A guy I met had brought it over from the UK with him and it still had the plastic parts under the chain cover and so forth that need to be removed before you use it, so I thought it was quite a good bargain considering I only had to pay the equivalent of about US$100 for it. The 16-inch bar wasn't ideal, and the size of the engine could have been a bit bigger but who was I to argue? I ended up spending days upon days and even weeks if I remember rightly cutting that stuff up and burning it. Gee those palm trees are tough and heavy. In fact, they are very heavy. After I dropped them I ringed them all up into carrying size but even the smallest of the rings that I cut were heavy. The biggest ones I could barely even move by rolling them, but I got there in the end and put them all into the middle in one big burn pile. It may have seemed like a waste at the time to pile them up and burn them but there was no one there to assist me with the carrying of them and it was hard enough trying to get them all into one central point let alone making piles all around the perimeter. Secondly, I knew that if they weren't cleaned up now while I was there it would probably never get done. Some of the local guys had suggested that over time they could pick away at it and slowly move the rings off to their cooking areas, but I knew it was going to take them forever which is why in the end I opted for my own strategy. So, a big burn up it was and by the time I was finished I'd done a reasonable job of getting it close to looking like a football field. Obviously, the stumps were going to present some sort of a challenge, but the locals reckoned they had a method for dealing with them, so I was happy to leave that part up to the experts.

After the completion of the football field, I was feeling like my body had been through quite a good workout. Probably because it was a good workout and not only that, but the scorching heat and sunshine had really been pounding down on me out there in the middle of that field. I was loving it, but it was tough. We helped them celebrate their school sports day a few weeks later and that was a great day but other than that I was pulled away with other distractions and so ended that little stint working at the school. It was a great introduction to that village schooling system and it had given me the opportunity to achieve something worthwhile early in the piece which I was happy about.

CHAPTER 18

SIERRA LEONE II

One evening I fell asleep upstairs on my bed underneath my mosquito net. It was a Saturday night and when I finally woke up the next morning, I simply felt drowsy and I just wanted to keep sleeping. I had intended to go to church that morning, but I quickly realised that there was no way I would make it. I let James know that I didn't feel up to it and they sent over a cup of tea and some bread. I downed the breakfast and fell straight back to sleep. That day I slept almost continuously through the entire day and night, only waking up to eat and then go back to sleep. James suggested that I might have had malaria which would have made sense because a while back I had stopped taking the doxycycline (antibiotic) which I was supposed to be taking to keep the malaria at bay. Anyway, by Monday morning I felt better again and so I got out of bed and continued working. The following weekend the exact same thing happened again except this time, instead of sleeping throughout one day, I slept two days without getting up. By this stage I realised James was correct and that it must have been malaria. I remember laying in bed thinking, 'well if this is malaria then this is quite pleasant'. Now I look back it does seem quite humorous, but the reality is malaria is by no means a laughing matter. I slept for two days and then decided I had better start taking the anti-malarial again, at least for long enough to clear up this current bout of the illness. The problem with malaria is that as you can see, the first time I got it I was not concerned at all because I felt quite cosy sleeping and enjoying the long rest, but then every time it returns the symptoms seem to get progressively worse. Symptoms can eventually turn very nasty with the sweats, loss of energy, stomach pains, bloating, indigestion, and then death. Approximately more than four hundred thousand people die of malaria every year around the globe and of these about seven thousand per year die in Sierra Leone. Malaria is a parasite that enters the blood through the mosquito bites and then proceeds to take over your entire system. Although it appears certain people in Africa have built up some form of immunity to malaria, most of the people that I knew in Sierra Leone would have to take treatment from time to time. The worst-case scenario is obviously death, but also in rare cases the malaria can affect the brain and cause brain damage, seizures or a coma. So, if you are lucky enough to be in West Africa be careful, and whatever you do make sure you have a way of treating such an infection should one occur.

Having finished the work at the school I spent the next week or two getting a lot of little chores done around the place. These chores included digging rubbish pits at the property where I stayed and at the orphanage across the road but this time, I was lucky enough to be accompanied by my friends who helped me dig. I think around this time we also concreted a floor at the missionary base where I was staying, painted one of the rooms and spent a fair amount of time cleaning up inside and out. We wheelbarrowed sand and aggregate over to the well in the orphanage and built up the area around the well plus the pathway leading to the well to beautify the area but mainly to try and raise the level of the ground so the water would no longer pool there and attract mosquitos. In the midst of all these goings on a visitor arrived from out of town one afternoon. The man was a tall, well-built and charismatic looking guy who stood out as soon as I saw him. He was a Sierra Leonean, with a quite dark complexion and a fantastic smile. Reverend Alusine Kargbo had come all the way from a town called Kamakwie in the far North of Sierra Leone. Over the years that followed I would become good friends with Alusine. Even as I write this book, I spoke to him yesterday on the phone and we exchanged messages this morning. I have a great deal of respect for these guys who grow up in such unforgiving life circumstances yet come out the other end still clothed in righteousness. How humbling it is to know such people, when I think of the minor inconveniences that I had to suffer as a child in comparison to what these guys have had to suffer as they grew up. It really does change the way you think about things. I am sure of one thing and that is that many of the men and woman of God that I met in Sierra Leone are surely better individuals than myself. I will happily admit this because for sure had I been born into their world I may never have survived.

Reverend Alusine Kargbo invited James and I to Kamakwie to attend a training program and crusade. After discussing the prospects of such an adventure and agreeing, we travelled in transport vehicles to the city of Makeni and then on motorbikes the rest of the way to Kamakwie. From Makeni we traversed vast expanses of palm tree forests, jungle, regrowth, and grasslands and still we were not even halfway there when our bodies began to ache from clinging onto the back of the bikes. What a trek and it was only going to get worse the longer the day went on. This definitely was off the beaten track and in fact the road had been dirt since the time we left Makeni. Luckily though it had been well maintained in many places and the red dirt surface actually made for quite a smooth ride in the areas that had been graded. We had our rests which helped and passed through some amazing small villages along the way. There are various checkpoints across Sierra Leone and nearly everywhere that you travel outside of the major city Freetown you are likely to encounter some form of checkpoint if not multiple checkpoints. Since we left our district, we had passed through a major one on the way to Makeni where police and military are stationed and then at least another two between Makeni and Kamakwie which were both smaller outposts only stationed by a couple of guys. Generally speaking, you won't have any problems when passing through these posts if you have the right paperwork and also if you're not a bad guy, which is what these checkpoints were initially put in place to stop.

Finally, we made it to Kamakwie and were welcomed by Reverend Alusine and several of the community leaders. What a day and what a place to be welcomed into. Again, some of the people you will meet in these faraway places will leave an impression on you for the rest of your life I can guarantee that right now. Cool people, cool place, great guest house to stay in and what a time we had. We stayed in Kamakwie for the best part of a week and while we were there, we participated in four nights of crusade with hundreds of people in attendance each night. The crusade was the result of several churches in the area putting their heads together to orga- nise a training course that ran for two weeks and catered for students who had come from various parts of the countryside including some from as far away as Freetown. The crusade coincided with the last week of the course and many of the participants were involved with the running of the cru- sade. The worship and celebrations went for hours into the night and could be heard right across town drawing many people to take part. Hundreds, if not thousands, at various stages were involved during the week. It's hard for me to explain too much about what I saw that week as I sit here now trying to put it into words. To say it was amazing is an understatement. For those readers who are believers I assume you may have heard similar stories as to what I recount so it will not be too much of a surprise. But, to those readers that are not of the inclination to believe in the spiritual aspect of the world we live in, each of you will have your own individual response. Some will disregard what I say, and some might be curious but one thing I know for sure is that if you were there with me and saw what I saw you would realise that inexplicable occurrences were happening in that place right in front of our eyes. Context needs to be given with regards to the spiritual world within Sierra Leone. There are varying reports as to the percentage of the population that claim to be either Christian or Muslim. My opinion is that roughly half the population would say they are Muslim, and half would say they are Christian. I cannot give exact figures obviously and there are varying degrees of the level of faith among individuals. For example, some are strong believers and perhaps you could say some would like to be strong but tend to struggle in their faith. That goes for both Christian and Muslim. But one thing I do know for certain is that most people in Sierra Leone believe in something. Nearly everyone believes in a God or the spiritual realm. I guess this is one of the good aspects about this country, because even if they don't believe in Jesus and the God of the Bible, they are aware that the world we live in is a spiritual world. This makes it easier to introduce to them the reality of Jesus. In contrast to this, one of the problems that we have in the Western world is that many people believe only in science and any concept relating to a spiritual world is nonsense to them. They are in essence programmed in a way that shuts down any opportunity that would enable them to learn about God. Sierra Leone and many other parts of the world are lucky in that although they may not be connected to Jesus they are in a state of mind where the introduction of Jesus is possible. So, Sierra Leone is blessed in that people are more open to learning. From the negative perspective, however, you could also say that sometimes this awareness of the spiritual realm has become a curse for many. The reason is that so many are involved in every other aspect of the spiritual world and not the Jesus as the Son of God aspect.

Sorcery is massive in many parts of Africa. Also known as black magic, voodoo, and traditional African religion, there are not many parts of Africa where sorcery is more commonplace than Sierra Leone. You could almost say that this part of the world is the capital of black magic. I'm sure most of you have your own ideas about what sorcery is and, in some cases, there have been romanticised versions of white witches and so forth passed around the globe, but the stark reality is that sorcery is not a healthy practice and in many cases I would consider it to be very evil. Yes, at the introductory level you might hear about seemingly innocent practices such as the use of jungle leaves for medicinal purposes but the further you delve into the various levels of magic you realise that the practices become more and more sinister. First up, using leaves and potions to cure sickness, then involving various spirits to assist with this. Okay, maybe that's just their way, who am I to say anything? Wrong, because that is not where it stops. It continues: love potions, potions to assist in the overcoming of anyone considered to be an enemy, potions to assist in the accumulation of power, curses to bring about the downfall of others, even the sickness and death of others. Perhaps somebody annoys you, then you might put a serious curse on them to make them go away. But the worst is yet to come, ritual sacrifice. Murder for body parts to be used in the creation of potions and curses. Sadly, many of these victims are children because it is often innocent blood that is required to complete the magical requirements and the only people considered innocent in this world are children. This is a fact: ritual sacrifice and murder for body parts is widespread right across the continent of Africa and likely the world. I'm sorry to say, this is not just a made-up conspiracy theory but real life. The evidence is right there should anyone choose to investigate. Court cases, convictions, reports, pending court cases, court files, police records, documented from one end of the globe to the other, reported by media outlets, common knowledge among the communities, and the list goes on and on. I cannot stress the fact enough, this is real.

Before I arrived in the area of Sierra Lerone where I lived, as many as five mutilated bodies turned up all around the same time in what locals called standard procedure in the run up to local elections. I do not want to go on and I don't want to tarnish the nature of this wonderful people, but it is true that very sinister occurrences are taking place among a small number of the country's inhabitants. The connection I am suggesting is that although this is the extreme version of the voodoo religion, it is in fact the same religion as the introductory level involving the jungle leaves and the invoking of spirits. The only difference between the various levels of sorcery is the outcome hoped for and subsequently the requirements for that outcome according to those who practice the religion. Basically, the greater the need the greater the input required. If you want to become healthy then that's not a big ask and just a small quantity of ingredients are required. However, if you want to become very powerful then obviously that is a much bigger ask and, what a coincidence, at this level you now need innocent blood. Welcome to the world of witchcraft.

For the readers that believe only in the sciences, this may simply be bad behaviour to you and granted it is, but I would suggest that not only is this bad behaviour, but it is also a very unhealthy foundation for life. Even in the lower levels of the religion, it can be said that these rituals of love potions, curses, accumulation of wealth and power rely on the manipulation of reality and others. Even if there is no actual real-world gain from these practices, the intent is there, and my belief is that such practises are self-destructive. I have mentioned in brief the worst-case scenario relating to these sorcery practices and this evil should be clear to all. From now on I'm not going to delve further into the discussion on religion and who's right and wrong because that is not what this story is about. I think that the best way to proceed is simply to state my belief and then leave the rest up to the reader. My belief is that the one true God which the Bible talks about is the original and true God. All questions relating to other religions can easily be answered once a person has put their trust in the one true God. Then I believe revelation will be received. There is also the other unmistakable evidence which reaffirms my belief in the one true God, which is that every other religion has unmistakable elements of darkness. I won't go on about it but if you consider such things as I have already mentioned and the other threads that run throughout other religions you will perhaps begin to gain an understanding of what I'm talking about. Threads such as ritual sacrifice already mentioned, cannibalism, teachings on murder and violence, fear, manipulation, hatred, male supremacy, hopelessness, condemnation, control and much more. These are the threads which disqualify other religions from being relevant in my opinion. Yes, it is true that some of the early war stories and circumstances written about in the Old Testament of the Bible are harsh but, put in perspective, the writings of the Holy Book in no way contradict the teachings of Jesus Christ. Contrary to critic's beliefs the 'harder to understand' aspects of the Bible represent the progression of time, development of humans and expose the ongoing cycle of sin prevalent among mankind. I think most importantly we begin to get a grasp of the absolute purity and majesty of the Almighty one throughout the teachings of the Bible. Sometimes I think people forget we are dealing with God. Completely perfect and powerful and one who makes decisions.

So, in summary, I believe other religions disqualify themselves and that the teachings of the Bible are true and correct. I believe Jesus is the son of God and the saviour of the world. I believe the Ten Commandments and the teachings of Jesus the Messiah are perfect and should be embraced by all mankind.

Back to our wonderful crusade in the far away town of Kamakwae. Unexplainable occurrences were happening in front of our eyes. Many of the people were celebrating, singing, clapping and full of joy. Stories were exchanged and testimonies were given. Though not everyone there that night appeared to be rejoicing. Due to the intense non-Christian spiritual practices that occur in some of these places, the locals will tell you that many of these people have spiritual attachments in their lives that sometimes manifest through their human flesh. According to the locals in this area, on this occasion we witnessed people like this. What we saw were the spirits in a wrestle for the control of that human body. As strange as it sounds, I can assure you that seeing this kind of activity in real life was even stranger. Have you ever seen how fast a large and powerful spider that's been hit with fly spray can move? That is what I saw that night only it wasn't spiders but rather humans and nobody sprayed anything on them or did anything to them to instigate this manifestation. Again, it is hard to explain but the spider reference does give insight into what was happening. For example, I saw several young women seemingly very strong and powerful literally bouncing off the walls and floor of this room with ease like some kind of insect. With an unbelievable acceleration they were able to bounce around on their backs, heads, legs, off the walls, up and down and around all without doing any harm to themselves whatsoever. I've never seen anything like it in my life. They were shaking, screaming, kicking, ripping their clothes and moving so fast few people dared to attempt to restrain them. Instead Christians stood at a distance and prayed for these people until eventually they calmed down and fell into what appeared to be sleep or rest. One of the weirdest ones I saw was a woman who seemingly grew in front of our eyes from the size of a normal, regular woman into a much larger, extremely broad-shouldered hulk. I can't say she actually grew but her physical presence definitely increased considerably. Her eyes bulged out of her head, and she hissed at us while she stretched out her arms to the night sky. I'm very rarely intimidated by anyone, but I've got to tell you this woman was scary.

I don't want to start to sound like a crazy guy telling stories. But the reality is I saw what I saw and there's no changing that. This stuff was really weird. I was there and I saw it. If I'm going to tell my story then I'm going to tell it how it happened. I continued to ask questions of the local guys, but the answers remained the same. These people had been involved in sorcery practices and what we saw was a result of that. I asked why nearly all the people were woman. The answer was that they are often involved in these practices from a very young age which is why they are more susceptible to possession. They also said that the woman are more open to supernatural experiences so when they come to a Christian crusade, they are open to the movement of God which then exposes these negative spiritual influences. Christians will tell you that when the Holy Spirit comes close to these women the unclean spirits resist which creates the physical manifestations we saw. Welcome to Kamakwae. Welcome to West Africa.

Our time in Kamakwae soon came to an end and as quickly as we came, we returned home. We left having made some new friends and these friends would remain on our hearts for a long time to come. After the Kamakwae journey things carried on as usual back in the Western Rural District. It wasn't long before I was introduced to a new church called the Jefferson Baptist Mission. This had originally been founded by an American church of the same name and the West African branch now comprised six branches in Sierra Leone and one in the neighbouring Liberia. I soon became friends with the senior Pastor whose name was Asa Conteh. After spending a small amount of time with Pastor Asa, he invited me to come and speak at his service on Sunday. I knew that I was still a rough guy at heart and that I had a lot of work to do in the future to refine my ways and become a better person. But I was encouraged by Pastor Asa's invite and his belief that I had something to offer outside of my usual skill set, so I agreed. As I sat at my desk in the upstairs room and tried to figure out what God might want me to say I prayed that I might be able to come up with a good message for these people. Immediately it came to me that I should speak about the Biblical disciplines. So that's exactly what I spoke about on the Sunday. I told them of the importance of reading the word of God, then meditating on the word throughout the day, prayer, worship, and service. This was the simple message I delivered. It was a safe message as well because it's pretty hard to get that one wrong.

Asa stood up immediately afterwards and said to the church, "Do you believe in the ability to hear from God?". Some of the congregation said "Yes" and then he continued. "Well, I can tell you that yes, we can hear from God". He then proceeded to tell the congregation that he had prepared a message for today in case I had not shown up to preach and that his message was the exact same message that I had just given. He pulled out his notes from his folder and showed them what he had prepared, and it was true that he had indeed prepared the exact same message as I had just given with basically the same headings and bullet points as mine.

I thought that was a very special moment. Pastor and I absolutely did not collaborate the day before that service began yet both of us had obviously prayed about a message and then gone ahead and prepared the same message totally unaware of what the other was preparing. Little moments like that can be a real encouragement, I think. It sure was for me.

Pastor Asa and I soon became friends and I met many of the church family and staff. I realised this was an awesome group and I trusted them. The Jefferson Baptist Mission from the outset had been well organised and structured. With the assistance from the American partners, the mission had a board of trustees, regular funding, and well setup premises at all their sites including the Liberian mission. There was also another non-profit organisation less than a kilometre away which was tied in with the Jefferson Baptist Mission. Up at the Dam there were a couple of American families who attended Jefferson. Between the Dam NGO and Jefferson Baptist Mission many overseas missionaries and volunteers were involved. All in all, this ended up being a very good connection for me, because it was through Asa Conteh and the Jefferson Baptist Mission that I was able to become a part of a circle of trusted people.

CHAPTER 19

SIGNIFICANT EVENTS, SIERRA LEONE

t wasn't long before I decided I wanted to permanently become a part of the Jefferson Baptist Mission. I realised that Pastor Asa would make the perfect mission leader for my upline manager. I needed that oversight in my life and, as far as the Sierra Leone immigration department was concerned, I also needed to have a sponsor while I was in the country. With this in mind, I asked Pastor Asa if the Mission could become my new permanent sponsor. Pastor Asa was happy to accommodate my request. From that moment I was reporting to and working underneath the banner of the Jefferson Baptist Mission.

It was also around this time that I moved out from the accommodation opposite the orphanage and stayed at a friend's house not too far away from the Mission. I didn't move far at all; it was still basically in the same area about a kilometre from Jefferson, but on the opposite side. All the time I was making new friends and gathering new connections. That first few months was a time of learning and setting up for the future. I met so many good people. Over time I began to understand how everything worked and who I could trust, which is also very important. By now I'd become a part of the Jefferson family. I had my friends from the orphanage, Kamakwie, and the Dam. I'd also developed friendships with numerous other individuals who were all involved in various types of activities throughout Sierra Leone and neighbouring countries.

God works in wondrous ways, as those who know Him can confirm. I had no idea what the future held when I went to Sierra Leone. While in New Zealand I had prayed for many different things, but by the time I went on my first mission to Africa all that I was concerned about was getting there and working hard to be of use to the Kingdom of God. That's really all I had in mind. During the first few months I used to spend a reasonable amount of time at one of the local charging centres. Instead of running a generator all the time and maintaining it, I had made the proposal to the guys who ran this charging centre that I would give them a contribution each day if they allowed me to use one of their rooms as an office and charge my electrical equipment while I was there. After they agreed, I spent many days in there plugged in while I worked on numerous newsletters and communications to the outside world. I did a lot of work in there and it wasn't just for Jefferson either, it was also for James my first connection when I arrived and numerous other small to large groups that had requested assistance. A lot of these people were working long and hard trying to build ministries and community programmes, but they simply lacked funding. One way to try and fill that need was to produce brochures and newsletters for them to send out. Once I'd produced something for them it was up to them to try and make it work. Raising money from inside the country proved to be challenging but worth trying. I guess in the end it all comes down to the person and what God chooses to do with that individual, but in the very least any assistance and encouragement we can give is not going to be counterproductive. As the bible says, "God works for the good of those who love Him," so let's do our best and see what He does with it.

While I worked away at the charging centre different people came and went. The guys that ran the centre all came from one family and they had their various friends and extended family coming to visit. One day a woman by the name of Saffie Marrah walked into my life. Saffie had a great smile and an outgoing personality which I picked up on straight away. She had a confidence about her that seemed to light up the room. I never knew that this would become a significant moment in my life but that's what it would turn out to be. Saffie would often pop in during the day and peer over my shoulder as I worked on my various assignments. Then, at different times she would go to the market for me and pick up items which I needed. I also met Saffie's family as she only lived a short distance from where I lived. For the rest of 2014 Saffie and I would remain friends. No matter what was going on I always seemed to run into her or get a text message from her even after all the events of 2014 unfolded. God was working on something here unbeknown to the two of us and only time would tell what that something might be.

Part way through the year a news headline broke that made waves right across the world - Ebola. A small number of people had been infected by the deadly virus over the border in Guinea. It quickly spread and soon people were infected in Liberia and right on the border of Sierra Leone. It wasn't long before Ebola had made its way into Sierra Leone but at this stage, I wasn't at all concerned that it would impact us hundreds of kilometres away on the edge of Freetown. My friend even asked me if I was afraid of Ebola and my response was that it was only a few cases and that those cases were miles away. I had no idea how quickly it would spread. Before long thousands of cases had sprung up across all three countries. Signs popped up all over the place warning us about Ebola and Ebola protocols.

Ebola headlines were on the radio, news, internet and everyone started to talk about it. Now I was starting to think we might have a problem. Ebola is a dangerous haemorrhaging disease that kills as many as 50% it infects. Symptoms include fever, pains, fatigue, and unexplained bleeding and bruising. As far as I knew from what we had heard about Ebola when I was younger, if you caught it, you were dead. So, I knew it was a killer, but I simply didn't know it would move as fast as it did.

By the time things began to get serious, I had shifted again. This time into a spare room at my friend's house. It was the most comfortable accommodation I had found since I first came to Sierra Leone. One of the difficulties I had faced was finding somewhere safe and secure to live. Obviously, I didn't want to spend all my money paying for expensive hotel rooms so I had opted to pay rent, but it simply wasn't as easy as you might think to find somewhere to do that. A lot of questions had to be asked before you decided on where you would rest your head at night. But for now, I had found a nice spot and it was still very close to Jefferson which I was thankful for. By now everyone was getting paranoid about Ebola. I remember going to the bank and standing in lines of people waiting for the cashier. Due to the heat everyone was sweating, and it is through bodily fluids that Ebola is most easily passed on. There would have been fifty to a hundred people standing around inside this small Ecobank and I'm sure we were all thinking the same thing. Gee I wonder if this was a good idea? But when things needed to get done you just had to do it, no questions asked. You just have to keep going. Another time during the outbreak I arrived at my friend's house only to find them lying in bed inside the small, shared pan-body (iron and stick) house in a terrible state. The other people who lived there were even afraid to go inside in case my friend had Ebola. My friend was shaking and absolutely fatigued due to the onset of a serious fever. None of us knew what was wrong and we only hoped that it was malaria or typhoid because that was treatable, but by now Ebola had spread right across the country and there were outbreaks all over the place including Freetown where my friend lived. There was only one thing I could do and that was take them to the hospital, so I said, "Get on the back of the bike and let's go". My friend climbed on wrapped in blankets and clinging to my jacket and off we went without a second thought. It turned out to be just malaria and typhoid, but not knowing that at the time I guess you could say that that was something of a risk to take. It was a risk that had to be taken though as far as I was concerned because if I hadn't done it that person might have died regardless of what the problem was.

That reminds me of an incident that happened with another friend of mine on a different occasion. I had offered to give my friend a ride into the junction so he could go and seek treatment for a skin issue that had been bothering him for some time. So again, we used the bike as transport and months later I found out that he actually had leprosy. I wasn't bothered at all because I hadn't gone out of my way to touch him, and I was also sure that God had my back with regards to these sorts of things. Be careful, of course, but also trust God.

The Ebola outbreak was a very intense time. It certainly was fraught for those who were directly affected by it. Approximately eleven thousand people died from Ebola during the 2014/2015 outbreak and many lives were destroyed. Nobody knows how many others died indirectly throughout the course of the outbreak due to other complications that were overlooked because everybody was so busy dealing with the more obvious problem. Thousands potentially died of malaria, typhoid, infection, and birthing problems, among other things, simply because the normal systems and procedures that would have saved them were now disrupted by the outbreak. God only knows what went on that the world might never fully understand but may those who died rest in peace, may God have mercy on their souls, and may God comfort the ones who were left behind.

By the time Ebola was in full swing there wasn't a lot I could do to help. I wasn't a medical person and at the time I had been putting a lot of effort into simply keeping myself and a few friends afloat. Money wasn't pouring in and with a tight budget came restricted movements and only the ability to do so much. The people I was staying with were also saying that if I wanted to continue staying there, I had to shut down all unnecessary movements and only go between the house, Jefferson and the necessary places like shopping and the ATM. I couldn't argue with that and so worked my life around their rules while I contemplated what I would do next. My uncle and heaps of people back home were pleading with me to get out and I was in two minds as to what I should do. I guess the option for me to try and get involved with the effort was a possibility, but then how much use would I be to them without the necessary skills and without the immediate connections and funds to stay afloat while on the frontline? I surmised that I might quickly become a liability to them rather an asset if I attempted to walk out on the tightrope from the place of safety where I presently was. That became my final decision which I stuck with. Stay out of the way and continue with the work at Jefferson while I wait on the Lord for the next move forward.

Looking back on that first mission to Sierra Leone certain memories spring to mind. Some good and some bad. Even with the bad I try to be positive about it and appreciate the good that can be taken from the situation. At times it's hard to work out what God is doing and why certain things happen. During these times I like to remember that He is the Almighty one with an extremely intricate and powerful mind that often I could not fathom even if I gave it my best shot. Testing circumstances call for trust on our behalf because He knows what He's doing. And sometimes the testing circumstances are happening to other people and not us and this calls for trust too. I remember flying down the motorway one time and I can't remember if I was riding or being driven but I recall a person's lifeless body lying on the island in the middle of the motorway. Nobody would even dare to go near them in case they had Ebola. I can only imagine that they may have laid there for hours until somebody from the Ebola response unit came to see what was going on. Perhaps they had been struck while trying to cross, I don't know, and I didn't go back to look either. Perhaps I should have but on that occasion I didn't stop. The thing about being in Sierra Leone is that everyday you will see people in desperate need and every week somebody will have an emergency and initially you try to help but soon you realise that you can't rescue everyone all the time. If you try you will bankrupt yourself and then there will be more people coming to you the day after. You can only do your best and help where possible keeping in mind that there will be weeks and months and hopefully even years in front of you, so you need to try and manage every resource you have including your energy. That is the way you must think. Of course, there are times when that all goes out the window and you must spring into action, but at least if we attempt to set out with this mind set it may assist in the longevity of our mission.

That would not be the last time I saw a body or bodies in Sierra Leone and now that I'm thinking back, I believe that it might have been a government order to not approach a body in case it was an Ebola victim. Whatever the scenario was the few times I did see bodies I either knew they were already dead, or I assume I realised it was not safe to approach them to find out.

The last couple of months of my 2014 Sierra Leone mission flew by and finally I decided to head out. So, with the assistance of my awesome friend Clark Hyland, we booked the tickets to fly me back to New Zealand. Things wouldn't go quite as smoothly as we had initially anticipated though due to the numerous flight cancelations. Because of the Ebola epidemic many of the airline companies were pulling out of the region and from memory I believe at least two of my planned departures were cancelled. While all this was going on I continued working at the Jefferson Baptist Mission and tried to keep out of harm's way. By this stage, after eight months of hard work and a few bouts of malaria, the thought of heading home for some Kiwi food and to replenish my bank accounts did seem rather appealing. But at the same time I was in two minds as to whether I should be staying, because after all this was the great adventure of a lifetime that I had been planning for some time. The thought crossed my mind that perhaps God wanted me to stay there, and I think that this notion could quite possibly have been correct, but I just needed a bit of time away to get my affairs in order again before I continued with the mission. The best place for me to do that was New Zealand where I could work and earn. Plus, my Uncle John was on to me about coming home because he was quite concerned about this epidemic. I wasn't too concerned, because for one I felt reasonably safe in the area we lived and secondly, I wasn't afraid of dying. At the same time I did not really want to die on my first mission. I know it sounds bad, but I thought, at least I should be able to complete a couple of missions here before I meet my Maker. With all this in mind we booked a third ticket to come out on another airline and then waited to see what would happen this time. It had been a wonderful experience and I would say that the most significant events that took place during those eight months were obviously the moments where God was showing me something and introducing me to people. The people were so amazing. I know that I have made lifelong friends from that first eight-month mission. There are too many to mention and so I can only reference a few like Pastor Joseph, Pastor Kemby, Jerome and Sharna who are Americans I met there, the Fullah boys from

Camp Junction, the orphans, and many more including the ones I already mentioned from Jefferson, Kamakwie and the various other destinations.

Saffie Marrah would also surely be a lifelong friend of mine I surmised. Or perhaps something more. Before I left, Saffie indicated that she had feelings for me. I really didn't know what to think and obviously I had feelings for her too, but the question remained as to whether they were in line with God's will. I had already committed to leaving and so any changes to the nature of our relationship would certainly be put on hold until I returned at a later date. So, we parted ways at the end of August 2014. I was definitely sad to say goodbye to Saffie and all my new friends, but at the same time I just had to keep moving. I think I knew that I would be back. I just had to tackle one obstacle at a time and the first obstacle was getting out of there with the numerous Ebola checks and usual obstacles associated with long distance travel along the way. As it happened everything went smoothly thanks to God and a powerful Kiwi passport.

As I walked out of the Auckland Airport back in New Zealand, I immediately began to feel disappointed. Suddenly it dawned on me that I was now back in the same boring New Zealand which less than a year ago I couldn't wait to leave behind me. I guess back in those early days of my faith I still struggled from time to time when it came to trusting God and I still wasn't in full control of my mind and what thoughts came and went. But I managed to keep on going and I guess on the bright side of such an emotion came the almost immediate desire to go back to Sierra Leone. That desire was reinforced as soon as I walked into the Life Church congregation in central Auckland a couple of weeks later. Still feeling a little down in the dumps, I headed into the service on this particular Sunday morning and as soon as I walked in there some amazingly powerful supernatural force came over me. There were perhaps as many as eight hundred people there that morning and they were all singing in unison one of the great beloved worship songs. I can't remember which one it was but the noise and power of the worship that morning reminded me of a British football stadium and in that split second, I was completely overwhelmed with emotion. Before I was even able to reach an available seat to sit down tears streamed out of my eyes uncontrollably. I didn't even know why, this had never, ever, happened to me before in my life and you know that from the world I came from you would never do this out of choice because I was taught to believe that men were tough. Men never show emotion. But I couldn't help it. I was struck by the power of the Almighty One and there was no way I had any control over what was happening. At first there were no thoughts, it was all just an unbelievably strong sense of emotion and not necessarily an unpleasant one at all either. Strangely enough, even though my eyes were filled with tears the feeling that came to me was a feeling of love rather than sadness. And then I began to think of all my friends I had left behind in Sierra Leone like Pastor Joseph and Saffie and Asa and everybody who had been a part of the process that would change my life for ever. Perhaps a little bit of sadness came in after I began to think about my friends, but for the most part it was love. This wonderful sensation lasted throughout the entirety of the service and even after the service I remember sitting with Pastor Neil Carter in the foyer with my back to everyone so they couldn't see the tears in my eyes. That truly was one of the strangest feelings that has ever come over me and to this day I would struggle to remember a moment comparable to that one. I think it was a definite sign to me that God had put this place, Sierra Leone, on my heart. It was through His strength that I was able to travel there, and it would be through His strength that I would travel back again!

Almost as soon as I arrived back in New Zealand I began thinking about my return to Sierra Leone and then planning it. I decided to head into the heart of New Zealand's agricultural land in the South Island and to put in a big effort during the upcoming busy season which would hopefully provide a good stockpile of funds for a second mission back to Sierra Leone. So, that's exactly what I did. I began the season by mowing silage for a local contractor and ended the season working on the Central Plains Water Scheme. By March 2015 I was boarding a flight to head back into West Africa, Ebola or no Ebola. As it happened Ebola was still around and almost seemed to come on with a bit of a surge in 2015. I believe the medical teams and international NGOs were coping a lot better by this stage and a lot of the systems by then were in place and saving many lives. The plan for me was to stay this time. I had decided that I would try and make this a long-term shift and establish myself in a way whereby I could potentially spend several years there. This would obviously entail finding work, possibly with an NGO or in one of the mines, and then continue with the volunteer/mission work on a part time basis. I had to have income though, because surviving on support from back home and what I had saved would only be feasible for so long. It just wasn't going to be enough unless I had a job. With that in mind, I knew I had to firstly deal with the immigration department in a way that allowed me to work and then find something to do.

After arriving back in Sierra Leone, I settled straight back into where I had left off working at the Baptist mission and catching up with all my friends. I was very happy to be back. We got quite a bit done in that first month and straight away I ran into Saffie again. She was doing well, and we began spending time together. Saffie had changed since I last saw her. I'm not sure why, but she just seemed to have this increased beauty about her. She and I had been messaging each other while I had been in New Zealand, and I hadn't put too much thought into any future developments. As soon as I got back, I had these feelings towards her that I couldn't properly explain. Like I was beginning to wonder if she was the one for me. I know it sounds crazy, but I didn't really have those thoughts in 2014 until while I was away. I had begun praying about marriage and I remember praying specifically that God would allow me to marry the right woman in my future and that I wouldn't marry her unless she was the right woman. Strangely the messages had continued from Saffie until I arrived back and then things just started moving very quickly. I was now drawn to her like never before. Was this the work of God I wondered? There were other considerations too that had entered my mind, for instance it had now been approximately four years or more since I had properly committed my life to God and the same amount of time now that I hadn't been with a woman. I had been celibate all that time knowing that to be a man of God I had to control myself especially in relation to intercourse. There had been women that I had spent time with, but I had been faithful to my commitment to God and had not overstepped that boundary. With a commitment like this come certain frustrations. I'm sure everybody knows it is not easy for a man to be without a woman for too long, hence the reason Paul in Corinthians suggested that we should marry if need be. I sensed that I was one of those people that needed to be married. And it's not that these desires are an evil part of us because, as we were instructed in Bible College, this desire is deliberately built into us by God for the purpose of procreation. But this built-in desire can cause something of an internal struggle when one is attempting to be a man of God out on the mission field where there's a lot of beautiful single woman. You can see where I'm coming from when I say I think it's a good idea for a man on the mission field to be a married man on the mission field. I really feared God and I didn't want to make a mess of things, and so I thought that marriage probably wouldn't be a bad idea. This was just one of the considerations that I had deliberated over in the last year or so. Another consideration which had to be taken into account was that I was now in my thirties, and I had begun to wonder if leaving things for too long might not be such a good idea.

Now as I said Saffie and I were spending a lot of time together and one day she had been over to visit me where I was staying at the time. She went to leave, and I watched her as she moved away along the walking track that wound its way off into the distance through the long grass and occasional building. Every twenty metres, Saffie would turn around then smile and wave at me before carrying on down the path. I'm not a big romantic but this moment struck a chord with me. She did this several times until her figure got smaller and smaller as she moved further and further away from me off into the distance. It was at this very moment in time that I realised that if I didn't marry Saffie now she would become another memory in my life like the people before her had become. She would become a memory that I would look back on with sadness, and I realised that I didn't want that to happen. As her figure got smaller and smaller as she moved away from me, so would her presence in my life if I didn't take this revelation seriously. I realised I had to marry Saffie.

I had prayed in the past that if I was not fully aware of God's plan for me and I was perhaps going to walk past one of His opportunities, then "Could He please take control and make His will come to be". I truly believe that God made this happen and within a very short period of time I sat with Saffie and asked her if she wanted to get married. Saffie said yes and so we began to put a plan into action. As I said I had this feeling that if I didn't do it now then Saffie would just become a memory. I knew that the best way for me to commit to this was to marry now, so that's exactly what we decided to do. After all I had decided that I was going to stay in Sierra Leone on a long-term mission now, so it just made sense. Within two weeks we had arranged everything and invited our friends and family along to the service. We were married on the 6th of April 2015 at the Jefferson Baptist Church of Waterloo, Western Rural District, Sierra Leone.

This day turned out to be one of the most significant events of my time in Sierra Leone and, as it turns out, of my life. In the years leading up to my commitment to following Christ I had hoped that one day I would have a wife and a family of my own. I didn't realise that it would be in the middle of West Africa, when I was supposed to be giving up my own life for the Kingdom of God, that I would be receiving from God one of the greatest gifts. Just as the scripture states, "For whoever wants to save their life will lose it, but whoever loses their life for me will find it" (Mathew 16:25 NIV). How much more precise could the scripture be? This to me is a true miracle.

Saffie and I rented a small apartment together as soon as we were married. We then set about putting a plan together for what we hoped would turn out to be a great start to our marriage. I should also mention Emma before we get too far through the story. Emma was my new daughter, Saffie's child who she had had as a teenager. Emma came into this world several years before I met Saffie and had basically been raised by her grandmother and extended family. When Saffie and I first got married it was decided that Emma would stay with her grandma until we were set up and ready to take her. Of course, her grandma had to be prepared to hand her over, because understandably her grandma had become very attached to the amazing young Emma. This gave Saffie and I the chance to be alone through the early stages of our marriage and I guess it wasn't a bad thing.

Not wanting to waste any time, as usual I soon got straight back to work at the Jefferson Baptist Mission whilst at the same time making numerous enquiries about possible opportunities to earn an income. Saffie had been a part of an Ebola response team prior to my return to Sierra Leone whereby they went around checking on individuals and households suspected of being infected with the virus. This was good for her at the time, but the money wasn't great and the two of us were setting our sights on something that would be a lot more favourable to our bank accounts. As an ex-pat in a place like Sierra Leone you will find you spend a lot of money just as I did. Unfortunately, it's just not as easy as setting yourself up the same way they do because our bodies are simply not used to it, and we need additional nourishment to keep us going. I found that I was spending a lot of money on fresh greens, salad, chicken, water, medicines, and the like. I just seemed to chew through the money and if I didn't keep it up then my body would quickly go into a decline. Perhaps that was just a phase I was going through. Now that I'm a lot older I may find my body doesn't need the same level of nutritional variety, but at this stage I certainly was mowing through the goods. I was also doing the work though. We had begun the construction of a four-room set of classrooms at the mission and that was hard work because the temperatures were soring and it was all done by hand; the whole lot. No power tools whatsoever. That went on for quite some time and nearing the completion of it I came down with a serious bout of malaria. I honestly thought I was going to die. Saffie and I had only been married for a couple of months and here I was totally knocked out in bed expecting that I would never get up again. I remember my mother-in-laws husband, who was a nurse, coming to our apartment and giving me a drip. I looked up at him and told him I thought I was going to die, but for some reason we were laughing at the same time. I'm not quite sure why it was funny because I was serious, but I pulled through and, no surprise, a week later I was back at work at Jefferson. Just had to keep moving right?

Apart from sickness, the work at the mission was going great. Now that the main structure of the classrooms was up and roofed, the floor had to be built up to the right level. The structure was built on top of a classic ring foundation and therefore the floors were still quite low and certainly uneven. This meant we had to bring in the dirt from elsewhere to build up the floors and then when they were up to the right level, we would concrete them. To solve this problem, I decided to dig a rubbish hole over the back behind the toilet block and so for the next three weeks I was below ground level with a pick and shovel digging by hand this massive rubbish/burn hole. As I dug down the red clay-like dirt was transported into the classrooms and slowly we brought the levels up to the right height. What a job. It just seemed to go on forever. There were also a lot of other little jobs going on in the background, as usual. Considering the tough environment we were living in, I was flat out busy most of the time. I also kept up the communications with home and tried to update the supporters on all the activities we were involved in, along with helping various individuals in the community who needed help. There was never a dull moment. The one thing I couldn't get on top of though was the hunt for paid work. Not on this occasion anyway. I even talked to several other ex-pat guys who had spent varying amounts of time in country and nearly everyone had the same feedback as the next guy. Very hard going, naturally most of the jobs are taken by the locals and those jobs simply don't pay. You're talking a couple of hundred dollars a month. I would literally spend that in a week easily. The diamond and iron ore mines were perhaps the most productive businesses in the country in normal times and would have likely been a good place to start looking, but due to the Ebola virus nearly every big company had virtually ground to a standstill. I was starting to get a bit worried because this was not looking good. Around about the same time Saffie came to me with some news that would change our lives forever. She was pregnant!

I could not believe my ears; I mean how did that happen? I had never in my life gotten anybody pregnant before and obviously I knew how that had happened, but I just didn't think that I was capable of doing that or perhaps certainly not as quick as that. I mean we had only been married for a couple of months. This was a real shock and hey, at the same time this was awesome, but I mean this changed everything and I mean everything. I was quite willing to take on the challenge of roughing it out in West Africa with my new wife and stepdaughter. But now we had a new-born on the way as well, this was getting a bit more serious, and this was going to take a lot of money. Saffie and I almost knew straight away that we were going to have to try and get the family back to New Zealand, but we gave ourselves some time to talk to our leadership and mentors before making any firm decisions. After the shock wore off, I was a happy man though. I now had my first blood child on the way to accompany my stepchild and this was going to be awesome. We had to trust God and just keep going no matter how difficult things might get.

CHAPTER 20
GOD'S FINISHING TOUCHES

Talking to leadership and family, everyone agreed that it would be the safest option if Saffie was able to give birth back home in New Zealand. So that's the decision we went with and thus began the next adventure of our lives. Again, it was in the month of August that I departed Sierra Leone on my own heading for home in an attempt to get Saffie into New Zealand before she gave birth. It was decided that Emma would remain with grandma for the time being which obviously grandma was very happy about. Saffie and I would go on ahead to get everything set up. Firstly, before that happened I would have to go ahead of Saffie, get a place for the two of us set up and do all the immigration groundwork before she got on the plane. I had a large workload ahead of me and I was up for the challenge, but unfortunately our plans would not go as we initially anticipated. Yes, I got back to New Zealand and set up a place for us to live. I managed to get Saffie a visitor's visa based on partnership. Unfortunately the two times Saffie went to fly out of Lungi airport at the end of 2015, and I believe the beginning of 2016, she was denied entry to board the plane due to differences in the interpretation of the various requirements each country had in place when it came to certain individuals flying. As I previously stated, flying on a New Zealand passport, no problem. But when it came to a pregnant woman flying on a Sierra Leone passport, not a chance. According to our travel agents in New Zealand, we were correct and Saffie had every right to fly but due to the way they interpret the law in Sierra Leone she wasn't allowed on the plane. In hindsight this was probably a good thing. Even though we had the meet and greet teams set up for her all the way from Africa to New Zealand, I now wonder if God was holding us up for a while so I could get a bit more time under my belt in Sierra. Also at the same time it was probably a lot safer for Saffie to be travelling with me the next time she tried, because when you go ahead and make that flight it dawns on you just how far it is. So, I think God had everything under control the whole time and again we just had to trust Him. Funnily enough you might be thinking 'well was all that a waste of time then, getting set up in NZ and getting visas etc. when I was going to have to go back into Sierra again?' and I think the answer is quite a good one and I believe definitely God's answer for sure. Where I set up in the South Island of New Zealand and prepared for Saffie to come to was an area where my mother's brother lived. Uncle John was an awesome guy, and it was during this time of setting up for Saffie that I was able to spend a good number of months with my uncle. He would only live another couple of years and left us in 2017, so had this scenario not played out the way it did I would never have been able to see him and certainly not for that amount of time before he passed away. I thank God for the time I was able to spend with Uncle John and I trust God that he is now in a better place.

Angus Asa Donaldson was born on the 29th of January 2016 at the Cottage Hospital in Freetown, Sierra Leone. I had my first son, and I couldn't have been happier. Angus was a strong, healthy young baby and Saffie was well looked after and safe throughout the procedure. I couldn't get back to Sierra Leone for the birth, but I knew there would be plenty of time to make up for this in the future because as we know God makes all things work for the good of those He loves. Later that year after getting Angus his New Zealand citizenship and passport, Saffie and Angus tried to fly again but met the same obstacles as before. Numerous different transit visas were required before she could board the plane and because Saffie was a Sierra Leone passport holder it was almost impossible for her to obtain these transit visas. I decided that God was drawing me back to Sierra and so I decided I would head back over there in time for my son's first birthday and have another go at the mission field before we carried on with the original plan of settling the family in New Zealand.

By January 2017 I was back in Sierra Leone just in time for my son's birthday. What a great time it was, and I truly felt blessed to be able to hold him in my arms for the first time. While I was away, an apartment had been built on Saffie's family property for us, so it was another blessing to be able to relax in what was quite comfortable accommodation by Sierra Leone standards. This was the beginning of another seven-month mission and as far as the success of the mission went it was probably getting up there as far as my level of satisfaction went. Over the course of the seven months, I worked for two separate British NGOs. The second project involved overseeing the construction of a birthing clinic in Freetown. This turned out to be a hefty project and what's more I was well-paid for it which certainly helped with the finances. Probably the most satisfying part of the working side of the mission for me was the large amount of street preaching that my friends and I were able accomplish. You see, right back at the beginning of my Sierra Leone story I had received the confirmation to go, in the form of the story of Jonah who was sent out by God to speak His message to the great city of Nineveh. I had this at the back of my mind the entire time I had been traveling to Sierra Leone and I thought well if that was my confirmation then maybe I should be following in Jonah's footsteps and speaking God's word to the people just as he did. In fact, prior to my return to West Africa in 2017 it had gotten to the stage where I began to feel that my missions to Sierra would never be accomplished properly unless I followed through on this part of the mission. So, when I arrived in 2017, I made sure that we spent a lot of time wearing out our shoes walking back and forward across Freetown and even as far away as Makeni speaking the word of God to those that would listen to us. We used loudspeakers to begin with, but then later found that it was more effective using my loud voice because there wasn't any distortion from the speaker. The message I spoke was a very simple message and I thought that it was a suitable one considering the background I had come from. I wasn't trying to reinvent the wheel or step outside of my level of expertise. I simply told them that they should turn away from the various activities that separate them from God, and fully commit to the one true God who the Bible talks about. I spoke the message in Krio, the language that all of them could understand and I repeated that same message without detouring from the main point. They all knew what I was saying as I referenced the various activities one by one and then encouraged them to turn to God. I finished by noting that the day for judgement will come. We spoke to literally thousands of people. Sometimes large crowds would stand and listen to the short message we spoke. I would walk and preach at the same time and then when we came across a suitable crowd we would stop and get as many people to listen as possible.

A tragic natural disaster occurred on the edges of Freetown in 2017 while I was there. The rains had started and had become so torrential that an entire side of a hill had slipped away and demolished everything in its path as it swept its way down the valley below. Over one thousand people died as a direct result of this mudslide and many more were permanently affected. It really was a horrible event. Within two days my friend China and I dropped down into the valley where the mudslide had taken place and with bags full of Bibles, we made our way down through the ruins talking to people as went and handing out the books. We made our way right to the end of the valley where the damage petered out and only evidence of flooding remained. From there we headed out to the hospital where a huge crowd gathered outside, and a local Freetown Pastor had set up a sound system and was preaching the word of God to those waiting outside. As soon as he heard what we were doing he handed me the microphone, so I took the opportunity to broadcast our short message to the crowd before moving on. A few days later as we continued to speak the word of God across town, I remember standing on the main road out of Freetown and watching as a large procession of military trucks carried the dead from the mudslide out of town and off into the distance where a large burial site had been prepared. It was a very eerie feeling as we watched the countless number of trucks rumble past us, and the smell of the dead wafted throughout the surrounding area. Many stood in silence, each person left to their own thoughts. I couldn't help thinking about God at this time and about what this all meant. God only knows.

The rest of my seven months stay sped past and before long I was preparing to head back to New Zealand to take advantage of the new working season. As I previously stated, despite the tragic loss of life in Freetown, it had been a good year for us. And I certainly had worn out my dress shoes as we walked for miles and miles across every part of Freetown and beyond. I was again aware of our money situation though. My decision to return to New Zealand hinged firstly on the fact that we had accomplished a lot during this mission and so I felt that we could now look to our next move. And secondly that we needed to keep moving and keep the ball rolling in terms of finances and future. By this stage we had rented a large house not far from the Baptist mission which was really comfortable. It was nicer than the apartment we had built on Saffie's family land simply due to the fact that it was much larger and was located behind the dam in a much more secluded spot. It felt good to be there and kick back and relax for a while after such a full-on year. I could only relax for a short time though because I had to keep the momentum going which we did end up doing successfully. I said my goodbyes to my beloved wife and son before boarding a plane at Lungi and heading home.

The plan was simple. This time I would arrange the New Zealand visa for Saffie whilst building up the funds again and, as soon as I could, I would head back over to help Saffie with the transit visas. Once we had the transit visas we would then fly out together with Angus. It all went according to plan. I worked in Kaikoura on the road repairing the damage from the earthquake, while our lawyer in Christchurch went to work organising the visa for us. The Kaikoura work paid well, and success with the visa came about in the first few months of 2018. This time it would work I was sure and so by mid-April I began preparing for my fourth trip over to Sierra Leone. I arrived back in Sierra Leone with about two and a half weeks to pull everything together. During that time I would need to be successful in acquiring three visas. That's one Chinese transit visa for Saffie, one for me getting into Guinea, and a third French transit visa for Saffie which we had to travel over the border to Guinea to get. That French one would be no easy task because we hadn't booked the required appointment and we were literally relying on God to make it happen.

God made it happen. Those two and a half weeks were quite a happy time for me because I had a confident peace about how this was going to work out. We got the Chinese and Guinean visa first and then the two of us travelled over the border into Guinea where we had to approach the French Embassy for an appointment. A few days later Saffie and I walked out of the French Embassy with all her documents in order. We had the transit visa, and this meant we now had everything we needed to fly all the way to New Zealand without any interference. It's quite hard to explain how much of a miracle this was, but let's just say that there probably isn't a country in the world that's as far away from Sierra Leone as New Zealand and I do believe that the only reason either of the embassy's took Saffie seriously is because I was standing next to her. There are other details as well like the fact that the website that we were supposed to make bookings for the French Embassy had been down for months and without that booking we shouldn't have been allowed into the embassy. God was on it though right from the beginning and everything fell into place just as we had planned. We arrived back in Sierra Leone with only a couple of days left to thank our friends for all their support and get ready to go. This time we flew out together. The three of us were finally on our way. Emma, Saffie's daughter and my soon to be adopted daughter, would wait in Sierra under the care of her grandma and my friends at the Baptist mission until we could make arrangements for her to follow. Obviously, that would be another adventure that would involve me going back to pick her up. In the meantime her grandma was quite relieved to have the only grandchild of her only daughter stay with her to keep her company while Saffie and Angus went ahead with me to get everything set up.

The three of us arrived in New Zealand on the 8th of May 2018. What an amazing time and to this day we thank God for everything He did for us. There are far too many little and big miracles that had happened in the seven years prior to our arrival into New Zealand and so I won't attempt to list them all now, but one miracle that I must write down is the miracle that many of you may find hard to believe. You see way back before I properly became a Christian when I was still up to no good in the city with my old friends there was something that happened which I can still remember to this day. It was perhaps around about 2008 or maybe even as late as 2010. I cannot exactly recall, but in any case, this particular night I was watching a movie at my friend's house, and it was an adventure movie about a guy who was in Africa. I left there that night thinking to myself how much I would love an adventure in my life. That night I prayed to God and in my prayer, I said "Please God give me an adventure. Give me an exciting adventure that would take me away somewhere so that I can do something amazing. Give me an adventure like the adventure I just saw in that movie". I can't remember the exact words, but it was something like that. Years later after I had been to Sierra Leone at least a couple of times, I found out that the movie I had watched had actually been set in Sierra Leone. The movie was the movie *Blood Diamonds* with Leonardo Di Caprio and the reason that I hadn't realised that it was set in Sierra was because it had been stated right at the beginning of the movie and I had obviously missed it. All I knew is that it was a crazy movie about some African country, and it had prompted me to go away and pray that God would do something like that or better than that for me. Wow, can you imagine this? Not only did God give me an adventure many times better than the adventure in the movie but He took me to the exact country where that movie was set. God answered my prayer precisely as I had asked him to and He did it years before I even realised He had done it. It wasn't until a long time after that I was sitting there, and I remembered the prayer I had prayed. Not only that but he had also answered another prayer of mine and that was to give me a wife. I think I had prayed for a wife even before I prayed for the adventure. Of course, I was praying about a wife sometime around the end of 2014 and the beginning or 2015 but that was not the same prayer I am talking about now that I prayed years before I even went to Sierra.

I know this all seems crazy and hard to believe but I can tell you now that one of my best qualities is that I tell the truth. I think I picked up this trait back in the day when I was hanging out with the old club guys, because back then the consequences of being a liar were so severe. So, over the years I think I just kept with that trait and later added to it with the word of God and the belief that perhaps even if I didn't have anything else I could be secure in the fact that I wasn't a liar. I always tell the truth and if I'm in a predicament where it's likely to cause a problem by doing so you will find that in that type of worst-case scenario, I am just not going to say anything at all rather than tell a lie because then I don't break one of the most important rules of the code which is, don't tell a lie. So, to put it simply, what you are reading here is the truth.

The year is now 2022. While many of my old friends from back in the day continue with their lives I too continue with mine. It is sad to have to say that a few have passed on into the afterlife, a few are in prison and others carry on in varying degrees of success or failure. For me, I am very grateful to God that He took me out and placed me in this new life that I was given. Otherwise, if He had not done that, I am sure it would be me who was either dead or in prison. But today I am alive thanks to God and his son Jesus Christ. I am still a little rough around the edges, but I can assure you now that what God has done in my life, transforming me from who I was to who I am now, is absolutely a true miracle. I am alive and I have been set free.

To date, my new friends who I met in Sierra Leone are now some of my best friends. It is so amazing that this whole new world was opened up to me. To this day Saffie and I continue our support back to Sierra Leone with our contribution to the distribution of Bibles in the country and our financial support to our home church, the Jefferson Baptist Mission. We also support, or remain in contact with, several other churches and individuals who God calls us to be involved with, such as our friends in Kenema, Kamakwie and of course Freetown. Emma will soon be my adopted daughter and we are hoping that not long after this takes place, I will be able to travel back over there and bring her to New Zealand. We are predicting this will take place in the next year. And gee what a shame now I get to go for another month or at least a half month mission back into my favourite destination Sierra Leone. To be honest I can't wait, and it is going to be so great to have Emma here with us. We are now all so much looking forward to the future because we know that God truly does answer our prayers.

As we wait on the Lord to finish off what He started I am happy to report that there is now four of us, five once Emma gets here. My second blood child was born on April 11, 2019, and her name is Margaret. She is a wonderful girl, and I am so proud to be her father. Angus is also doing great and the four of us live together in rural Canterbury. I am employed by a local transport company that mainly services the agricultural sector and Saffie is doing a great job as a mother. She is also hoping to expand a small business which she has been experimenting with over the last couple of years. As we continue with our plans, we try to bring God into the centre of all things. My awesome mother, Catherine, is still alive, so it is wonderful that our children are able to enjoy spending time with their Kiwi grandmother and some of my other relatives. Who doesn't agree that aunties are amazing? Mine certainly are, which is why I'm so grateful for their input into our lives. We remain in close contact with all our friends here and overseas. This provides us with a sound Christian fellowship which we all need when trying to navigate this life. And yes, in the future once we have set up a solid foundation here in New Zealand, we do want to continue with mission trips back to our beloved Sierra Leone and perhaps even the greater West Africa. But that will be a story for next time, right? You bet. There is one other piece of good news to mention before I sign off, and that is that it's entirely possible that one or possibly a few of my old club friends might be able to find their way in the direction of the cross too. But again, that might be a story for next time. The Lord has been so good to us. I know that He will do this for anyone that comes to Him. God bless.

CHAPTER 21
UPDATE

The year is now 2025. I had an opportunity to work on the book again briefly, so I decided to add an update. I can confirm that God has continued to look after us well since I finished my book. Infact, almost immediately after submitting my book for publication in 2022, I traveled back to Sierra Leone to pick up Emma our daughter. What a fantastic trip away it was, with about three weeks over there. I was able to catch up with all our friends and family and completed about two weeks worth of missions work. Reverend Kemby and I traveled to Kamakwie for a number of days and the remaining time we spent in Waterloo with the Jefferson Baptist Mission and the various other friends and contacts we have there. We spent a few thousand dollars on the members of the congregation at the locations we went and helped a few individuals out too that we came across in our journeys. Finally, Emma boarded a plane with me and we arrived in New Zealand near the end of 2022. What an awesome time for all, especially Saffie and Angus who had been missing Emma since they left Sierra Leone in 2018.

Upon arriving back in New Zealand we have carried on with general work and the financial support over to Sierra Leone. Saffies business had to take a back seat for a year or two though while she went through the pregnancy of our fourth child, Gordon Alan Donaldson. Gordon was named after our oldest friend Gordon Dennis and my father Alan Donaldson. Gordon Alan Donaldson is now two years old and he is doing exceptionally well. We expect that Gordon will develop into a serious man of God. I know this will be the case. The other children are doing great but are just a few years older.

We still live in the same area but we have slightly larger accommodation obviously to cater for the new arrivals and we have been doing some extensive planning for the future. Everything is going well. I'm working with friends presently and eagerly waiting to see what God does next in our lives. The next move is likely to be another short mission for me back to Sierra Leone to take care of some more family and church business. And following that, we know God will be doing some amazing things.

To the readers, thank you from the Donaldson family and until I get a chance to do another update, God bless you all and God speed in whatever you are doing.

ACKNOWLEDGEMENTS

There are so many people who have helped me along this journey that it really would be difficult to mention everybody. I mean, nearly everyone I know has helped in one way or another. Friends, mentors, people I have worked with or for, church associates, college associates, my African friends and colleagues. The list could go on and on. So realistically I cannot name every person because I would be here forever but I can say that those people who have been involved in our life journey have all played an important part and so I thank them for that.

Above all, God has been there for me through the best and worst of times and my greatest appreciation goes to Him. God is great. Jesus is Lord and the wonders never end.

To my wife Saffie Donaldson, thank you for being so wonderful and patient throughout our time together and while I have been writing this book. To my children, thank you for being awesome and putting up with a dad that spends most of his time at work or on his computer. I love you, my family.

My dear mother has been there for me from day one and in spite of my harsh and sometimes objectionable behaviour she has never stopped caring for me. Thank you mum.

Thank you to Saffie's mum Zynab who has looked after the family and many extras along the way. We love you.

Some of my early friends, who went through their own trials as well, also helped shape me into the person I am today. And I appreciate the help the old president and his wife gave me when I really needed someone to be there for me. Thank you. Even to this day when I reach out for feedback and advice you're still there.

As I moved into the realm of a new life my Christian friends like John Wilks and Reuben Edwards were often there in support. In particular I need to say thank you to the late Alfonsus van Wamel for his Christian influence on my life and also his wife Kathy who up until this day still lends her support from time to time.

I also really do need to thank those guys and ladies up there at Lifeway College in Snell's Beach who helped me through the first period of my new life: Pete Meafou and Pastor Reuben Gwyn; Christina and Caleb Wylie; the College librarian, Eleanor Neil; Malcom Collier; and all the numerous other friends I made during my time there.

Whilst in Africa I made some amazing friends and so many of them helped in so many ways. Pastor Asa Conteh, Pastor Hassan Mansaray, Pastor Alusine Kargbo and Pastor Joseph Sennesie are just a few of the many I need to mention but to these guys and to everyone else who played a part thank you very much. Special thanks to Pastor Asa for marrying Saffie and I and then continuing to be an integral part of our lives throughout the various projects we have embarked on.

To my church family in New Zealand, thank you. To the sponsors who have played such an important role along the way like Clark Hyland and Doctor Ross Fountain thank you. Gordon Dennis thank you. Aunty Margaret and the rest of my relatives thank you. Everyone who knows us and who does life with us we couldn't do without you. Thank you.

Special thanks to Eleanor Neil for putting in countless hours of work on this book and helping to shape it into the finished product that it is now.

Above: Old Motorcycle Club in Christchurch, New Zealand. Early 1990's.; *Below:* My friend and I, early days in Christchurch. I would have been in my early 20's.

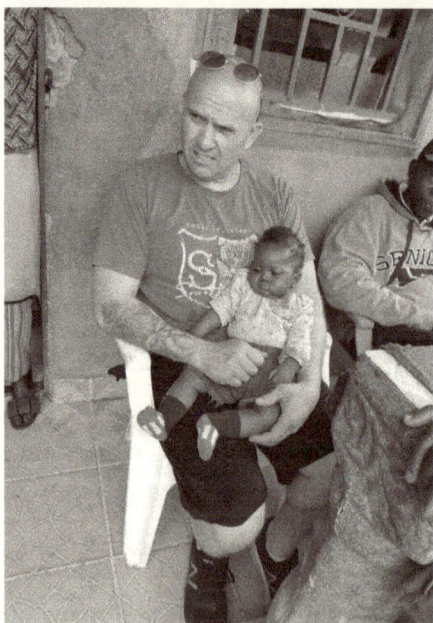

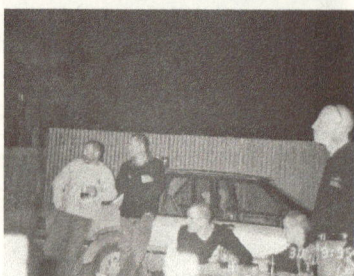

Clockwise from top: Old Motorcycle Clubs at Ruapuna Speedway, Christchurch, mid 1990's; My 21st birthday party, Hornby, Christchuch, I am second from right; My friend and I are seated with one of the local babies, Sierra Leone 2022.

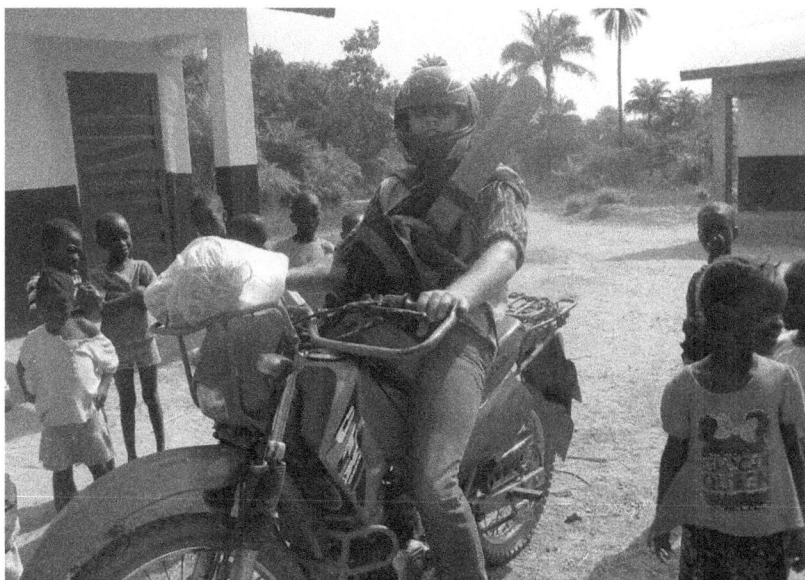

Above: Above: Loaded with chainsaw and day bag I arrive on site at a school associated with the mission to clear a football field out of the scrub for the children, early 2014; *Below:* Handing out rice and supplies to those in need during my 2022 outreach to Kamakwie, Sierra Leone.

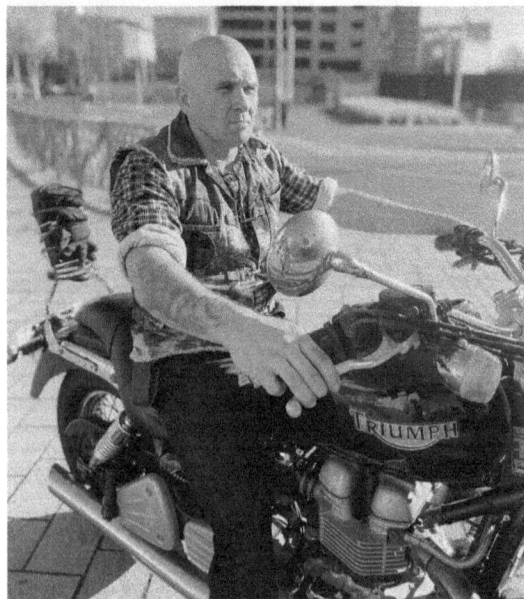

Above: My wife and I on our tenth wedding anniversary, Christchurch, 2025. *Below:* Me on my bike, 2022.

Above: My family and I, including young Gordon on my wifes back during a recent trip to Mount Hutt, New Zealand.
Below: Some of the team and I during my 2022 visit back to Sierra Leone.